Catch Them B(

MW01068510

In this exploration of a radical approach to the psychoanalytical treatment of people on the verge of mental breakdown, Christopher Bollas offers a new and courageous clinical paradigm.

He suggests that the unconscious purpose of breakdown is to present the self to the other for transformative understanding; to have its core distress met and understood directly. If caught in time, a breakdown can become a 'breakthrough'. It is an event imbued with the most profound personal significance, but it requires deep understanding if its meaning is to be released to its transformative potential.

Bollas believes that hospitalization, intensive medication and CBT/DBT all negate this opportunity, and he proposes that many of these patients should instead be offered extended, intensive psychoanalysis.

This book will be of interest to clinicians who find that, with patients on the verge of breakdown, conventional psychoanalytical work is insufficient to meet the emerging crisis. However, Bollas's challenging proposal will provoke many questions, and in the final section of the book some of these are raised by Sacha Bollas and presented in a question-and-answer form.

Christopher Bollas, PhD, is a psychoanalyst practising in London.

Sacha Bollas, PsyD, is a psychologist practising in Los Angeles.

Catch Them Before They Fall

The Psychoanalysis of Breakdown

Christopher Bollas
with Sacha Bollas

Routledge
Taylor & Francis Group

LONDON AND NEW YORK

First published 2013
by Routledge
27 Church Road, Hove, East Sussex BN3 2FA

Simultaneously published in the USA and Canada
by Routledge
711 Third Avenue, New York, NY 10017

Routledge is an imprint of the Taylor & Francis Group, an informa business

British Library Cataloguing in Publication Data
A catalogue record for this book is available from the British Library

Library of Congress Cataloguing in Publication Data
Bollas, Christopher.
Catch them before they fall : the psychoanalysis of breakdown /
authored by Christopher Bollas, with Sacha Bollas.
p. cm.
1. Mental health consultation. 2. Mental illness--Prevention. 3.
Psychoanalysis. I. Bollas, Sacha. II. Title.
RA790.95.B65 2013
616.8917--dc23
2012030396

ISBN: 978-0-415-63719-0 (hbk)
ISBN: 978-0-415-63720-6 (pbk)
ISBN: 978-0-203-06954-7(ebk)

Typeset in Garamond
by Saxon Graphics Ltd, Derby

Contents

Introduction

People seek psychoanalysis or psychotherapy for many reasons. Few do so in order to have a breakdown, even though some are barely hanging on. While consciously seeking a talking therapy in order to work through what are tamely termed 'relational issues' or 'situational problems', many are in great private mental pain, unable to imagine surviving life.

Psychoanalysts have come to realize that if an analysis takes place several times a week, and if the analysand regresses to dependence in a rather ordinary way—lessening defences, opening up the self to interpretive transformation, abandoning disturbed character patterns—the self will usually break down in a slow and cumulative way that is not traumatic. This is how many psychoanalyses work, and for the most part standard analysis needs no supplement of any kind.

There are some clinicians who, usually as a result of being attached to a psychiatric hospital, have a special interest in working analytically with psychotic people. Otherwise, most analysts see a range of patients and only occasionally come into contact with psychosis or with someone on the verge of breakdown. Usually, any potential catastrophe can be mitigated through conventional psychoanalytical work, but occasionally this proves not to be the case.

This book is devoted to the challenges posed by working with people in therapy or psychoanalysis who, either suddenly or gradually, indicate signs of breakdown that, for various reasons, cannot be met by an ordinary clinical approach. It suggests an alternative route to the customary paths taken— hospitalization and/or anti-psychotic or anti-depressant medication—which can impact on a person for the rest of their life.

Furthermore, this book is intended as a riposte to the much celebrated CBT or DBT treatments which, in effect, enable the patient to sideline their internal life by diverting attention to a time-limited cognitive project. Just as a parent resolves a toddler's crying by diversion—'Oh, look at that over there!'—such interventions may forestall a *necessary* crisis, or trivialize the deep function of symptomatic behaviour.

If the patient's breakdown distils crucial psychic issues that are now open to change because of the self's vulnerability, the analyst's lack of an adequate analytical response constitutes a crucial failure to meet the self's needs. When this happens the analysand may halt the breakdown, guided by new axioms built upon the assumption that the self's needs are unworthy of being met, or are too excessive to be coped with. The breakdown then becomes *structuralized* as a permanent fault within the self, that is, in my view, nearly impossible to remedy in later analytical work, whether with the analyst concerned or in a future course of therapy or analysis.

Diversion through CBT/DBT will shallow out the self and, for a while, seal over the cracks, often to the relief of the patient, the hospital statistics and the State, which is preoccupied with the cost-effective self. But for those who understand breakdown as a profoundly human experience, distracting a self from the meanings of their frailty produces a particular new form of loss. It is too soon in this century to know the long-term effect of such superficial treatments, although I take the position that it is irresponsible to let time tell. People in breakdown do not need to have someone avert their gaze from the internal world to a self-help homework book; they need to be heard and understood from the depths of the self that are presented to them and that constitute their crisis.

What follows must be seen in an appropriate light. The vast majority of people with whom I have worked in my career have been 'ordinary' patients, who were suffering for different reasons, who could talk about it, enact it in the transference, and with whom conventional analysis was the fare. So it is important to point out that this book presents highly unusual circumstances. The majority of analysts may never encounter the type of situation addressed here, but it is not so unusual as to be unworthy of consideration.

From time to time, maybe once every few years, I would find that a patient seemed to require something different from me. I am not referring to particular diagnoses. In my first year of private practice, I had three psychotic patients in five-times-a-week analysis, but the fact that they were manic or hallucinating was not a surprise; it was a regular feature of their presentation. I am referring to those comparatively rare occasions when a non-psychotic person indicated, through altered presentation and behaviour, that they were beginning to crack up.

In Great Britain it was required of non-medical psychoanalysts, such as me, to telephone the GP to inform them that their patient was in difficulty. The doctor would see the person and most likely recommend hospital care. I was fortunate that the first time this happened, with a patient that I shall be discussing in Chapter 4, I was familiar with the GP practice. I asked if they would allow me to provide increased psychoanalytic sessions in order to see whether we could keep the person out of hospital, and they agreed.

So I first offered her more sessions within the working week and then, when this did not seem to be sufficient, I increased the sessions to twice daily, seven days a week. This continued for three weeks until she emerged from her crisis. I knew this was unusual, but I thought then that it was a one-off.

In fact, some years previously, I had wondered what I would do should a patient of mine need acute care, and I visited the in-patient units of several hospitals in north London. I thought about how I could, if necessary, take a patient to the hospital, and I found a local minicab firm that was reliable and kept their number in my consulting room.

In conversation with a much respected colleague, a GP with psychiatric training whom I shall call Dr Branch, I realized that it would be possible to form a team of people to provide a holding environment for a patient who became psychotic or was having a breakdown.[1] The idea was to offer a type of psychoanalytically-informed care that would obviate the need for a patient to go into hospital, and I also discussed this with my Area Team Social Work leader and his colleagues. During the late 1970s, Dr Branch provided medical back-up as I worked with schizophrenic and manic depressive patients, and when they were in acute trouble we collaborated in ways that prevented hospitalization.

It was not until my second decade of practice that I began to notice a pattern: some people, at certain times, seemed to need a special form of psychoanalytical treatment if one were to meet their clinical needs and not fail them. By the mid-1980s there had been a number of occasions in which I had responded to a patient's impending breakdown by increasing their sessions.

By then I had also supervised many cases abroad where therapists and analysts had tried to do something similar. However, there was a key difference: these clinicians usually offered the patient an extra session here or there, and only when it was too late. In other words, they were providing reactive treatment, not proactive care. Furthermore, they were tending to communicate their ambivalence towards their own actions to their patients, thus unknowingly fomenting greater anxiety that soon turned into a vicious circle (patient and analyst making one another increasingly alarmed) that often resulted in hospitalization.

The outcome of a breakdown is not necessarily a descent into psychotic decompensation, although this may occur. More commonly, people who suffer a breakdown, which is not transformed at the time into a breakthrough, become what I term *broken selves*. They then function in significantly diminished ways for the remainder of their lives. They may be diagnosed as schizoid, schizo-affective or chronically depressed, but in fact they demonstrated these signs only after the breakdown. I believe that there are many people who present the picture of a chronic character disorder when actually they spent months in a state of desperate need. It was a time when their core issues were manifested but received no effective therapy. In my view this is a tragedy on a large scale, all the more so for having gone largely unrecognized.

In the late 1980s, I went a step further in extending psychoanalysis. Owing to the gravity of one patient's need, I offered sessions that lasted all day. Radical though this venture may seem, at the time the decision seemed natural and correct in light of the severity of the person's imminent breakdown.

I did not know at the start how long we would meet on this basis, but it proved to be three days, from 9 a.m. till 6 p.m.

A few years later, a similar situation arose, this time with a once-weekly psychotherapy patient. Again I offered all-day sessions, and again we met for only three days, and this has proved to be the case on each subsequent occasion. As I now work a four-day week I was, with one exception, able to meet these analysands on a Friday, Saturday and Sunday, resuming our ordinary schedule the following week. In all these situations the person returned to their former session times.

It was striking that, in addition to dealing with the patient's acute crisis, the three-day sessions appeared to substantially shorten the subsequent analysis. Each patient who went through such a breakdown worked with me for another twelve to fifteen months, but not longer than that. These remaining months functioned as working-through periods leading to termination and, as far as I know, none of these people has sought further analysis or psychotherapy.

From the beginning, I felt convinced that these breakdowns were potentially generative. I knew from my work with schizophrenics and manic depressives that their hospitalizations had been devastating, and I did not want to lose my analysands to hospital and mind-numbing medication. I knew this was the time when the person most needed analytic help.

Importantly, I had worked with a number of non-psychotic people who were in five-times-a-week analysis, and who—I realize now, looking back—were in the early stages of a breakdown. Weekends became unbearable; as Fridays approached the analysand would go into retreat, and would remain traumatized for a day or two the next week. (I would term these people my 'Wednesday analysands' because this was when they would recover from the break). Such situations would prevail for months before the pain subsided and the patient morphed into some other state. In hindsight, I feel that I probably failed them by not offering extended sessions.

As time went on, my experience was telling me that the psychoanalytical process was, in itself, so efficacious that one *should* allow it to be modified for a person in dire straits, with extended sessions, increased frequency or, occasionally, with all-day sessions. I believed that the analytical experience itself functioned as a third object which could be the vehicle of transformation.

Of course, none other than Freud himself had argued that some analysands required extended sessions when clinical needs could not be met within their normal hours, and in British psychoanalysis there is a long and complex history of taking disturbed people into a deeply regressive analysis. For Michael Balint this meant reaching the area of the 'basic fault'; for D.W. Winnicott the aim was to get to the 'kernel' of the self through the abandonment of false self-defences.

More than any other analyst in the UK, Winnicott experimented with extended sessions in which he encouraged analysands to go into regression, and this was common knowledge at the time. He and the analysand might agree some months in advance when he would be in a position to offer this, and it would enable the patient to postpone the breakdown. I will indicate later the ways in which I disagree with Winnicott's use of regression, but I could not have envisioned working in the way I did without this tradition, which had existed in British society for over twenty-five years.

In addition, pioneering work was being accomplished by R.D. Laing, Cooper and Esterson at Kingsley Hall and, later, by Joseph Berke and others at Arbours. Both Arbours and the Philadelphia Association have operated houses for the treatment of severely ill people for over thirty years, and continue to do so.

The mandate for writing this book emerges from two sources. One is my view that psychoanalysis is the treatment of choice for patients who are breaking down. Although received wisdom tends to be that it is effective mainly with those who are psychoneurotic, or who have high levels of functioning, in fact plenty of psychoanalysts work with severely disturbed and psychotic analysands, and know from experience that interpretive work at the core of a person's ailment can be deeply transformative. Indeed, when the person is at their most vulnerable—and especially in breakdown—they are usually particularly amenable to help, and to the development of insight into the self.

The second reason for writing this book arrives out of the responses I have encountered when presenting this way of working to groups of psychoanalysts over the years. In formal group presentations there has been almost uniform disapproval. The most commonly held position is that it violates the frame, is seductive, gratifying to the analysand, or that it constitutes an enactment within the transference and countertransference that goes unanalysed.

There have been concerns expressed over the professional and ethical propriety of extended psychoanalysis, and suggestions that allied professions (psychiatry, psychology, etc.) might well oppose such intensified treatments. It is also argued that by not immediately utilizing psychotropic intervention or hospitalizing the analysand the person's suffering will be prolonged. In fact, while it is true that those people in additional extended analysis did suffer considerably at the time, once the breakdown had been passed through their suffering was greatly relieved.

I knew, both from my own practice and from hearing many case presentations, that analysts who stuck to the five-times-a-week model, without offering additional sessions, not only inadvertently prolonged their analysands' suffering but ossified the breakdown. In these cases, a breakdown did take place, but instead of leading to a renewal of the self it became a wasted opportunity. The analysis might then continue, often for many years, without any transformative change and, too often, the analysand was destined to become just another broken self.

A very different response, not usually encountered in formal settings but common in small group clinical discussions, was: 'So what else is new? Don't we all do this?' Indeed, analysts would discuss work, of an apparently similar kind, whereby they had offered patients additional sessions.

While I obviously found this response more heartening, I was often left with the feeling that such ready agreement tended to preclude examining the issue in more detail. I have already mentioned that, in most cases where an analyst had provided additional sessions to people who were having a breakdown, it was with mixed feelings, provided with too much hesitation, far too late in the game, and too few. However, the fact that many psychoanalysts and psychoanalytical psychotherapists feel impelled to offer extra sessions at moments of crisis implies a recognition that the intensification of analysis is a legitimate course of action and, in a sense, the work I am describing here simply builds on that as a matter of common sense.

The move from the addition of a few extra sessions to offering two sessions a day, seven days a week, and especially to working with a patient for the whole day, does clearly take things a significant step further. I feel, therefore, that my own theory and practice requires greater explanation so, encouraged by colleagues, I made the decision to write down and publish the lectures I had given on this subject, in order that what I believe I have learned could be put into the public domain and become an object of thought.

From time to time I shall be referring to the contrast between the American and the British treatment of people who are breaking down, and the fact is that there is a huge difference in the creative latitude in these two cultures. American clinicians have to contend with far more intrusion into their practice than do the British and Europeans, although I know personally a number of American psychoanalysts who have forged ahead, working with their patients in defiance of professional, regulatory and legal strictures.

In Europe, clinicians are freer to exercise their own judgement based on purely clinical considerations, and so are less driven to tailor their practice to regulatory responsibilities. They are, therefore, in a better position to see someone through a breakdown than their American counterparts. Sadly, in Britain today, 'evidence-based' mandates are threatening to lead to the 'manualization' of psychoanalysis but, until now at least, European analysts have been relatively free of State intervention.

In this sense this book is a testimony to the past. Whether it can be relevant for the future depends on the success of psychoanalysis and the therapies in convincing the State to refrain from dictating therapeutic praxis.

Even with the more open European attitude towards the treatment of breakdown, I have not written about my work with extended analysis until now. As I have said, on the first occasion when I experimented with this approach I reckoned it would be a one-off experience, unlikely to occur again in my career. It was only over time that I realized that a different clinical dimension had entered my practice and that I should give it consideration.

At the start I was hardly confident about extended analysis. There was no real precedent for it in this form, and I had doubts as to whether this work would prove truly mutative or whether it was simply a form of 'transference cure'.

Also, I did not want to become known in London as some sort of 'regression analyst', to whom colleagues would refer patients, specifically for this sort of work. As I shall discuss, people who *consciously* seek a breakdown as a desired event are, in my view, most unlikely to benefit from this extended work. In addition, I did not want my patients to know I worked in this way as, for some, it would have seemed too special, too alluring. In these circumstances it would, undoubtedly, have elicited transferential confusions and interfered with their analyses.

For a long time I did not discuss this work with any of my colleagues. At first, I saw no need for this; these seemed to be isolated events and I just got on with making my own adaptation to them. Later, as I became aware of the emergence of a different way of working, I was reluctant to present what I knew would be treated as a matter of controversy. I found the clinical task absorbing and challenging, and somehow it felt very private to the team of people with whom I collaborated. It was clear to the doctors, psychiatrists, social workers and others that we were engaged in an extension of analysis, and the reflective work seemed best done amongst ourselves.

With all these reservations in my mind, it was only towards the end of the 1990s that I felt I had gathered sufficient experience in this area to venture to present the work to groups of colleagues. I first spoke of it at the Seminar for Psychoanalytical Candidates, run by the late Helen Myers at Columbia University. It was met with respectful surprise, some shock, but real interest. Even so, it was another ten years before I presented it again, in a series of lectures: at the Chicago Workshop on Psychoanalysis; the annual Arild Conference in Sweden; and finally, in 2010, at the Franz Alexander Lecture at the New Center for Psychoanalysis, in Los Angeles.

This book is both a report on some of the clinical dimensions involved in this practice and a discussion of the theoretical considerations. It traces the development of my adaptation to these clinical realities in such a way that the reader will, I hope, see the logic of the developing technique, and its implications for practice and further study. I have tried to indicate where I made mistakes of judgement and what I learned from them. I have no way of knowing how many other analysts have followed a similar path, but perhaps this book may serve as a meeting place for those who have worked with extended analysis in times of crisis.

I am grateful to all those people who commented on these presentations and, in various overt and subtle ways, encouraged me to push on with this book. I am well aware that the text will raise many issues in the mind of the reader. Sacha Bollas has collated the more frequent questions posed over the years and they are presented in the final chapter, in the form of an interview.

I owe a special debt to the late Otto Will Jr, for many years Medical Director and, in effect, Director Emeritus, of Austen Riggs. While I was Director of Education there during the mid-1980s, he would visit for several weeks at a time and I had heard that he would always ask to be notified whenever one of his psychotic patients was breaking down. He would walk over to the 'Inn' where the patients stayed, and would sit for many hours with the patient. He did not want to resort to medication, or to transfer the patient to a secure unit; they would see the crisis through together. We met several times and I discussed with him the work I was doing in London. He immediately grasped the clinical challenges I was facing and was very supportive. He did warn me, however, that I should never expect my colleagues to understand, much less approve of my deviations. Be that as it may, and whatever the outcome of this publication, I am very thankful to him for listening and supporting me in my explorations.

Also, my thanks to two psychoanalytical colleagues: Dr Arne Jemstedt, for his careful reading of the text, and Sarah Nettleton, for her meticulous editorial work. I should make it clear, however, that the views expressed here are solely my own.

Chapter 1

Broken selves

Psychiatrists, psychoanalysts, psychologists and those working in the field of mental health have developed nomenclature over the decades that identifies people according to types of disorder. Even though there is pressure to adopt one manual across all the professions—*DSM IV or V*—psychoanalysis has its own classical diagnoses: hysterical, obsessional, schizoid, depressive, and so forth.

The underlying assumption is that a person can be fundamentally defined according to a particular character type; that they have always been this way, their psychodevelopmental fate determined by a combination of innate mental structure and those axioms developed during early life. And for many people, this is true. However, analysts often find that once they get to know the patient the initial diagnosis of hysteria or schizoid disorder seems to be of limited value. As the analysis proceeds, with the intrinsic therapeutic efficacy of the analytical process, a single disorder becomes a complex psychodynamic picture. It was Wilhelm Reich who argued that character disorders were like frozen psychodynamic puzzles that, when analysed, would reanimate. The character armour established by the person would dissolve under intense psychoanalytical interpretation.

In other words, if a person has formed his character gradually, over a long time, then through analysis his defences and character positions can be analysed and transformed. It is not a question of miracles. It is long, difficult work which may result in varying degrees of success – and failure.

Not until recently, have I realized that in my own practice I have missed something rather obvious. Sometimes when I see a new patient present as, for example, schizoid or depressed, what I am actually noticing is that something seems to have happened to that person; they seem to be a broken self. By 'broken self' I am not referring to a specific diagnosis, nor am I suggesting a new category of pathology. The term is intended to apply to a broad spectrum of people, including those whom we would call 'normal'. The only common denominator between them is that they have had a breakdown, often in early adulthood, during which they were left without adequate therapeutic care. Whatever the travails of their childhood, or the inherent weaknesses of their ego or their mental structures, it is this breakdown in adult life that has left a distinguishing scar upon their being.

I came to discover in what ways these people differed from those with traditional character disorders as I supervised many cases in different parts of the world. People who have previously suffered a breakdown—that may have been predisposed because of schizoid, depressive, hysteric, or obsessional patterns—present a greater challenge than usual to clinicians.

Over time it seemed to me that certain patients, typically arriving for therapy in their thirties or forties, could not respond to analytical therapy (or anything else) because they had simply given up on life. They were without the sort of organized Mafia gangs within the self, described so astutely by Rosenfeld; they had no such edge to them.[1] Therapists would describe working for years with such people, to no end other than occasional expressions of gratitude. For the most part the patients were functioning way below their capacities, often intermittently unemployed or in positions substantially below the level suggested by their academic achievements. The analyst or therapist usually presented the person for supervision because it was a matter of despair for them in the countertransference. They saw nothing efficacious taking place and questioned whether there was any point in continuing the work.

Gradually I came to see that there was a pattern to be found amongst these people: a great many of them had suffered previously from non-psychotic breakdowns.

Some of these can be precipitated by external trauma. The breakdown might occur at university, going unnoticed in the shuffle of agitated circumstances that come with life in that environment. Or, after graduation when a person would expect to enter the workforce there might be a series of rejections and, after a struggle to keep pushing forward with life, a collapse. Or perhaps a relationship that had endured during student years ends suddenly, leaving the individual abandoned, bereft and unable to recover from the loss. Or maybe a parent, sibling, or close friend dies, leading to a catastrophic grief.

More often than not, however, the precipitating event is something so subtle and seemingly innocuous—a credit card being declined, a parking ticket, an unkind comment by a stranger—that only through analysing the *unconscious* meaning of the event can its toxic effect be understood.

Whatever causes the onset of the crisis, those in attendance fail to meet the person's needs adequately during the breakdown. If the person is in therapy they may be unable to afford an increase in sessions, or the anxious therapist might refer them immediately for medication, anxiety management or group therapy. All too often this is followed by a period of hospitalization as the patient's crisis deepens.

At this point the breakdown becomes structuralized. The personality reforms itself around the effects of breakdown, reordering the self in order to function and survive under significantly reduced circumstances. This heralds a meagre future existence.

This restructuring of mental life means that axioms by which the person has lived are altered. With a mental breakdown of this kind there is a shattering of one of the core assumptions instilled by a good-enough childhood; that when we are in need we will receive help. Various new assumptions take its place:

> It's best not to seek help from any other.
> If I am vulnerable, I must kill off feelings.
> Only a fallback position can be safe.
> I must disinvest in the object world and abandon a relation to reality.
> I will give up on ambitions, plans, hopes and desires.
> I must find people who are in a similar situation and live within a new society of fellow broken selves.

A broken person is characteristically indifferent to their life. They are passive and resigned to their situation. In that they have decathected from their object world one might think of them as aligned with the death drive, but they lack the force of hate, envy, denigration or cynicism that is so often seen in characters that inhabit the hell of the death instinct. Their indifference may be accompanied by unrealistic plans—writing a novel, becoming an entrepreneur—but no actions are taken towards accomplishment in their field of dreams. Instead, these plans function as projections of the broken self: broken dreams that exemplify the impossibility of success.

The broken person's affect is significantly reduced. They rarely show emotion and are not driven to anger, anxiety or euphoria by events in life. Instead, they maintain a steady remove from affective shifts; nothing is worth the effort.

They may identify with celebrities that they see as having fallen on hard times owing to some negatively transformative event in their life. Such interest is significant as it stands out in a mentality otherwise uninterested either in politics, cultural affairs or environmental issues, or in diet, physical fitness or anything to do with the self's health. The fallen celebrity seems to be a reflection of the person's own catastrophe.

They do, however, have a hidden ideal self. It lives on in the unrealistic dreams of success, but it also functions as a defensive imaginary companion, as if the person is trying to hold on to aspects of the self that existed before the breakdown. Winnicott might suggest that the false self is protecting a remnant of the true self. I think this hidden self is a ghost; a sad representative of what the person had thought they could become. Psychotherapists and analysts working with someone who is broken can feel annoyed by this object relation to the ideal self, with its unrealistic, grandiose expectations. Occasional impulses towards achievement—purchasing a book on writing a novel, or surfing the Internet in search of business ideas—are never pursued for long. And it is important to note that such dreams are not accompanied by enthusiasm, but are stated as if they can be realized easily.

When the therapist makes an interpretation there are various typical responses. Often the patient does not reply, is silent for a while, and then continues to talk as if nothing has been said. If confronted they may reply with 'I don't know' or 'maybe', showing little evidence of introspection. Instead, they perseverate about someone at work who is asking too much of them, or recount how they are planning a holiday but are unsure where to go. They radiate a low-level mental pain, a quiet depressive despair, but show no interest in what this might mean. It is purely evacuative.

Although the patient remains detached in many respects from their therapist they adhere to 'the therapy' or 'the analysis'. I have come to understand this as a fear that they will have another breakdown and, therefore, need to be connected to a therapist as an insurance policy against future trauma. These patients form a kind of neutral transference to the clinician, one that expresses their negative restructuralization, and analysts feel that they are treading water and getting nowhere.

Almost all clinicians with whom I have discussed these people argue that this is a form of attachment to a non-human other, and they will reach for terms like 'autistic enclave' or

'Asperger's' or 'psychic retreat.' I suspect that the increasing prevalence of the diagnosis of 'mild Asperger's' may include some people who acquired these characteristics only after a breakdown that reshaped the self's mental structure.

A common reason why breakdown results in a broken self is the use of psychotropic intervention. Although such medication may help relieve the person in the immediate situation, the ingestion of such drugs negates meaning. Discovery of the unconscious reason for the breakdown, and the opportunity for sentient understanding and tolerance of it within a human and therapeutic situation, are denied to the person. The patient may visit the doctor for repeat prescriptions, they may see a psychiatrist briefly every few weeks, but all this does is to seal over the structuralized breakdown and unwittingly ensure its permanence.

Many 'serial patients'—people who continually seek different forms of therapy—bear the scars of breakdown throughout their lifespan. They may appear as depressed, with relational difficulties, problems with motivation and a generally lacklustre interest in cultural object use. When they present to their therapists they often have a deep conviction that it is too late to gain help, or they may make unrealistic demands that therapy work right away, their subsequent disappointment causing them to abandon the treatment, or to move from one therapist to another, in which case the scars of breakdown are projected into the abandoned clinicians, who are given an intense experience of being dropped by the other, left to get on with life bearing a wound within the self.

When I realized how many people fell into the category of broken selves I wondered if and when this had occurred in my own practice. Several people came to mind.

Tim had come to a clinic where I worked following a break-up with his girlfriend. He was desolate and in deep trouble, and had been on sick leave for several weeks. Still, he was a highly cooperative patient who entrusted me with his feelings and his existential crisis, and we had reason to believe that he would emerge from his breakdown. I had the opportunity to increase his sessions, which I did not do, and indeed I left the clinic about a year after we began our work. I learned later from colleagues that he continued to attend for a few months after I moved on, and then he left.

Seven years later, I received a phone call out of the blue. Tim wanted to visit me. He did not want to resume therapy; he simply wanted to meet up. The man I encountered was a broken human being. Although he had a job and was in a tenuous relationship with a woman, the signs of life I had seen in him years before were all gone.

I think too of Lila, a woman in her early thirties who came to me for five-times-a-week analysis. I saw her for four years before she moved to another country. I have etched in my memory a period of several months in the second year of her analysis. Ordinarily an articulate and reflective woman, now she was unusually agitated, and could not gather her inner experiences into speech. I knew she was in difficulty but I stuck to our pattern of five-times-a-week analysis. I have little doubt now that a breakdown was taking place and that, had I offered her additional sessions, she might have been reached and her life changed. At that time it simply did not occur to me.

By the early 1980s, however, I was determined to change my practice in working with people on the verge of breakdown. I did not consciously connect this to work with Tim or Lila or other previous patients, but unconsciously I must have been aware that I had failed them, and that something else was needed.

Chapter 2

Signs of breakdown

Psychoanalytical work has as much to do with how the analyst *receives* the analysand as with what they say to them.

If the analyst has worked with a patient for a year or more they will have begun to internalize their character form. It is hard to define this, but think of how after listening, over some time, to the music of a particular composer we begin to feel within ourselves the shape of their musical personality. Our unconscious receives, organizes and recognizes *patterns*, and these patterns constitute the form that any content may take, whether it be a musical idea, expressed in the pattern of a particular harmonic and melodic idiom, or a poet's idea taking form in the rhythm of their characteristic syntax that shapes the sequence of images.

Psychoanalysts are trained to be 'impressionable'; a term Freud used many times to describe the way the analyst registers the analysand. They allow a person's way of being and of relating to affect them. They need to be as open to this as possible and even though they may begin to notice patterns early on, they should suspend early judgements in order to continue to be open to the form of a person's character.

When the analyst's unconscious communicates to the patient's unconscious that the other is open in this way to character communication, the patient will become more expressive, often more difficult, certainly more specific in the release of personal idioms of being and relating, and over time, the psychoanalyst will begin to feel the shape of the patient within themself. Just as we can conjure the feel of Mozart within our consciousness, even when we are not listening to his music, we know the feel of the many impressions created by the impact of the patient.

The sort of receptiveness assumed here is, however, not characteristic either of psychoanalysts who regard it as mandatory to be constantly interpreting the transference in the here-and-now, or of those who enter into a dialogue with the analysand, offering the analyst's personal response to what has been said. Both these approaches offer a very different type of analysis from that based on neoclassical principles, and I want to emphasize that understanding this book, and certainly contemplating using the ideas presented here, will be highly problematic for clinicians who work in either of these two ways.

That is not to say that analysts working within those traditions do not have strategies for working with patients in breakdown, but my own work, within the Freudian tradition, operates from the crucial assumption that the analyst must be quiet and recessive for long periods of time, in order that the analysand's free associations and character moves are offered ample freedom to articulate themselves. If psychoanalysts are actively interventionist then these associations will not establish their patterns of meaning, and the person's character will be absorbed by the analyst's construction of the transference, as the selected object of focus.

Within the context of Neo-Freudian classicism, the psychoanalyst engages in a negative capability; they suspend their own views and immediate responses, in order to facilitate the incremental establishment of the analysand's idiom of being. Within this interformal context, if the analysand unconsciously introduces a nuanced difference from their idiom of being it will be registered by the analyst.[1] This registration will be subliminal to begin with, but as it repeats itself over time the difference will assert itself as a pattern, and this will raise a certain signal anxiety in the analyst, rather as though a snippet of Brahms were to appear in the middle of a Mozart sonata.

Let us move on now to think about the forms of breakdown with which the psychoanalyst may be confronted. To oversimplify somewhat, there are two fundamentally different types: one in which the analysand shows warning signs – hints that they may be coming apart; and another that is acute and has no preceding indications.

Take the first kind. Assume for a moment that, from the beginning, the patient has been vulnerable and the analyst is well aware that a breakdown is possible. The analytic process itself, especially the invitational evocativeness of the transferential experience, will elicit an easing of the self's ordinary defences. There may be a transition period as the old self releases itself into breakdown progressively, and this may last days or weeks. At first, the person seems bewildered, as if something is up but it cannot be identified. There may also be a temporary dissociative stage in which the person is somewhat outside the self, in a state of derealization, or observing the self from a psychic distance. There is a growing feeling of helplessness as simple tasks—answering letters, putting petrol in the car, doing the laundry—feel increasingly impossible.

One of the most customary early signs of breakdown is a slowing up of ordinary patterns of speech. Most analysands are hesitant or silent from time to time, or convey doubt about what they are saying, but what characterizes breakdown is another kind of hesitation, in which the cessation of speech can be a result of the intrusion of an odd idea, or the emergence of powerful but inarticulate feelings, a weakening of the ego, or the first waves of an *après-coup* (deferred action). It does not seem to be the result of psychodynamic conflict caused by a specific idea that the person does not want to talk about, or the experience of facing fearful mental territory or troubling transferential feelings. It is a hesitation that seems forced upon the patient. Something is going wrong.

'I don't know' or 'I just feel a bit strange' are typical comments in response to analytical inquiry, but with a patient on the verge of breakdown this is expressed in an unmistakably different way. In addition to a change in vocal inflexion and mood, the analysand may also move differently. They seem hesitant in the way they walk to the couch, lie down and walk across the room. They seem preoccupied, absent-minded, not fully in their bodies. They may knock over a table or stumble; instead of sitting in the waiting room they may stand, looking lost.

Indeed, a very common sign of emergent breakdown is a self in this 'spacey' state, staring into the middle distance, accompanied by unusually long periods of silence. This is seen especially in adolescent breakdown, when it should be taken with grave seriousness as one of the most significant indications of an imminent decompensation, especially if it follows an obvious blow in the self's relation to their peers.

Most importantly, the psychoanalyst will sense a shift in the patient's idiom. The patient's form within the analyst's unconscious is now changing, and it is this registration that will alert the analyst to the analysand's predicament, often before the indications mentioned above are observable.

At moments like this the analyst's reaction is crucial. Noticing something is different, they will feel uneasy and anxious. This signal anxiety is important; it should prompt the analyst to take the actions that are essential to reach a patient before the outbreak of severe breakdown. They will already be making unconscious adjustments to the patient's new patterns in being and relating. Even if these cannot yet be voiced, they are learning something new that will eventually be available for comment and for potentially life-saving interpretation. Whatever the signs being given by the analysand, it is vital that the analyst provides additional psychoanalytical coverage before the patient becomes helpless.

The second type of breakdown occurs quite suddenly with no apparent transition period. This happens most often with patients who are highly vulnerable but rigidly defended.

In this situation it is crucial that the analyst discover in detail what has happened in the previous days that could have precipitated a mental catastrophe. There will always be such an event, but I have never known a patient who wanted to describe it. The analyst therefore has to be ready to hear the word 'nothing' stated many times.

Here we come to the first significant digression from ordinary analytical technique. The analyst, who rarely asks questions, must now become inquisitive. This fact in itself brings to the analyst's presence a therapeutic agency that is experienced by the patient as different, even unprecedented, and highly effective. It is as if the analysand's denial is met by therapeutic intensity on the analyst's part: they become the 'detective' to which Freud often likened himself.

When discussing free association Freud stated that the most important material was that which seemed least relevant. In my experience the best course of action is to ask the patient simply to give an account of what they have done in the last few days. 'Just tell me what you did over the weekend.' Inside the narrative of the recent past there will have been some seminal event, often seemingly innocuous, that has upset the patient and they do not know why. It is hugely valuable, rather like the *Ur* dream of the individual's ego that, if unravelled, will initiate a network of empathic interpretive understanding that will prove profoundly important.

Belinda came to her session on a Monday. Clearly something was different about her; she seemed to be in trouble. I was unable to discover from her that day what it was that had caused her to feel differently about things, but on Tuesday she told me said that on the Saturday, when she had been to the market to get her favourite carrot cake mix, it was not there. She had been planning to make this cake for a very special friend, she could see it on the shelf in her mind's eye and when it was missing she could not believe it. She searched the entire store for the cake mix, asked the staff to find it for her, and no one could account for its absence. During this experience Belinda felt herself cave in. She went to a bus shelter outside the shop and sat down in a daze. She felt that everything was ruined. She had other things to buy and chores to do but she couldn't summon the energy to do them.

In a moment like this it is vital that the psychoanalyst allow the analysand a great deal of time in which to recover *thoughts* that are attached to the event. This information-gathering is crucial to what will follow. We should note that at this stage it is not affect that is needed, but information. Asking a person how they feel is non-productive and will produce limp abstractions.

If this is difficult to imagine, think of the pre-adolescent child. He comes home from school with a changed expression and heads to his room without a greeting. Something has gone wrong. It might be tempting for his worried mother to rush up to his room, barge in and ask what has happened. But an attuned mother will give the child some time to recover before knocking on the door. 'Go away' means, 'Not yet'; 'Come in' is a beginning.

'So, what's up?' may be a good way to approach the problem, but the usual response will be 'Nothing'. If she waits, after a while tears may roll down his face, he might bury his head in the pillow. The good-enough parent will still leave the child in peace to collect himself before he can tell her what has happened. More often than not this leads to a long period of talking and the child will recover, feel healed and be ready for life again.

Likewise, the psychoanalyst must wait until the analysand is in a position to talk, and if it seems that this may take longer than what remains of the session, then the appropriate measure is to provide more time. Time is the crucial variant in how well one can help a patient who is on the verge of breakdown.

Belinda recalled that she had wanted to make carrot cake because her friend had said that she loved it, and had not had a good one in a long time. My patient knew of this perfect box of cake mix but she did not know how to make carrot cake from scratch, and she was anxious. Would her friend like this cake or would she sniff at it, leaving her feeling humiliated?

The dinner had taken place on the Sunday. It had not gone well from a culinary point of view. Moreover, Belinda's altered state was observed and this caused her husband to be critical of her. 'Whatever is the *matter* with you?' he asked after the guests had left. She could not explain. She crawled into bed, numbed by events that she could not understand.

The unconscious, being what it is, had taken her to the wrong shop. The cake mix was not there because it had never been there. It was a parapraxis, a bungled action which, as we were to discover later, was her way of protesting against the fact that she had set herself up to try to give her highly critical friend something precious. The carrot cake was a metaphor for her. She was desperate that someone she genuinely loved could see something lovely in her, but her friend was highly narcissistic and had never been overtly affectionate towards her.

What distinguishes Belinda's parapraxal act from an ordinary psychoneurotic event was the degree of *mental pain* evoked by this happening. These signs of serious distress are characteristic of the individual who is coming to breakdown. It is as if the mind is in anguish because it cannot process its urgent thoughts and anxieties, leaving the patient disabled. Close behind the mental pain is an acute state of loss and grief: the person's recognition that they are losing the capacity to think comes with the conviction that they have therefore lost the self.

Later, we would discern in the 'carrot cake' a phonemic fault line that bore meaning. 'Carrot' contains the sounds 'care' and 'out', although the 'out' is almost silent. Unconsciously, Belinda was searching for an object that she knew her guest would not care for and that her effort would therefore fail. In making the carrot cake she was creating a moment when her effort of care would be rejected. (Later, she heard the word 'garotte' in 'carrot' and thought that she might also be preparing a dish that would strangle her friend).

The most common precipitator of breakdown is a quarrel with a friend or sudden rejection by a partner. These common phenomena can evoke latent psychological issues that rush into the void created by the rejection, and fill the space with deferred affect, usually stemming from a much deeper and more disturbing event in the self's childhood. This has the immediate effect of regressing the patient, because higher level adult functioning is usurped by the psychic position of the self at the time of the originating event. If the patient cannot speak and goes blank it is most likely that the trauma now emerging is arriving from the pre-verbal period of the self's life. It cannot be put into words. Part of what they know about themselves, but have never thought, is now appearing through a dreadful transformation in the nature of their being.

At this point, the self is suffering from the arrival of a frozen memory. It is impacting on the self, there is regression and loss of some functioning, but the ego is still together. However, if a good-enough other (the residue of the mother) does not arrive in this moment to help the self by providing an auxiliary or supplementary ego, then loss of ego functioning is very likely. This brings very disturbing changes: the inability to focus on work tasks or the demands of ordinary life; a failure to recollect recent events, thoughts that seem odd and off-centre. There may be an inability to hear what other people are saying or to collect words into coherent sentences.

These and other manifestations of ego disintegration create primary anxiety. The self realizes that it is losing control of mental life, the capacity to carry out tasks and the ability to relate. It is losing its way of being.

Before discussing the defences against primary anxiety we should take a moment to contrast this with 'signal anxiety'.

Signal anxiety is a specific response and, as such, is different from 'free floating anxiety' which is around, to some extent, most of the time, disconnected from its original source. If you are dressed in a red shirt and have to cross a field in which you suddenly discover there is a resident bull, your anxiety will rise. This is a valuable affective state as it alerts you to the fact that you are in danger and need to take action.

Signal anxiety usually has to do with a specific and limited threat to the self, but that threat need not be external. In the early stages of a mental distress, if the self has an odd symptomatic outbreak, such as an inability to recall recent events, poor judgement or a feeling of dissociation, the ego will set off an internal alarm. This alerts the self that something is not right within its mental life and that help is needed. If they sense this kind of alarm many people will turn to a friend to say they are feeling strange, or they may seek therapy.

Signal anxiety is very common in adolescence, a time when great intensity of feeling is coupled with emotional immaturity. Young people may feel unable to turn to friends and family, interpreting the anxieties as fateful forecasts of mental breakdown. If this pressure becomes unbearable an adolescent may even commit suicide.

Primary anxiety occurs after signal anxiety has failed to perform its function. It is not a warning, but a form of panic that arrives in response to the sense of helplessness brought on by loss of ego functioning. It is so strong and so terrifying that it sets off powerful defences, as if the self is engaged in a last-ditch effort to ward off breakdown.

When people come to hospital in this state, clinicians are usually witness to the defences constructed against primary anxiety. The most common of these is the apparent loss of affect. It has, in fact, not been lost; it has been cast off in order that it may not be experienced. Another common defence is stilted or rhetorically mannered speaking, as if the person is reading from a telephone book. Another is a false congeniality aimed at keeping others away from intrusive questioning and deflecting their efforts to help.

All of these defences are forms of partial withdrawal.

If these higher level forms do not work to mitigate primary anxiety then the person will take more radical steps, such as withdrawing from all contact with people. This is seen most commonly in clinical depression but it also occurs with people in breakdown when they sense they are losing ego functioning. One alternative reaction is agitated depression, when the person seems quite the opposite of withdrawn; in fact, they seek out people to talk to and are garrulous, constantly discussing the problems that beset the self.

This compulsive talking may be interpreted by clinicians as an outbreak of OCD, but it is actually an attempt by the mind to displace reality with a mental alternative; to take over the world of reality with the world of thought. Whether the breakdown has been owing to an external or an internal event, the agitation is a result of a structural failure of the ego to cope with the intrapsychic impact. By finding others to talk to, the individual is trying to escape out of their own mind into someone else's, but this attempt at projective identification fails because the source of the anxiety is endopsychic. There will be an inevitable return to the self's panic.

If the person continues to be agitated there are potentially dire consequences. By overspeaking the self, the person evacuates the mind of its contents, placing them into the many people who, by listening and trying to be helpful, have unwittingly colluded in the process of breakdown. Overspeaking results in the loss of the self's ability to learn from its own unconscious free associations, as thoughts are offloaded and worded out of existence.

In addition, this outsourcing of the self's thoughts by projection results in a *psychotic democratization* in which the hierarchy of meaning is lost. One idea is as significant as the next. Without such a hierarchical order the self is without a mental rudder; there is only one direction and that is circular. A psychotic vicious circle is established in which the person goes endlessly round and round and round. Sometimes they may feel that they have grasped something, but nothing is retained and no understanding is achieved.

If the self continues to be emptied of its mental contents, the process of thought itself deteriorates, and the self now relies upon others to think its thoughts. By now, this may be a disparate group of people who do not know one another and can, therefore, have no coordinated, collective thought process. In a matter of days, this can lead to *psychic dehydration*, the drying up of mental life. The self is now just a voice. Thoughts emerge at a fast pace but with no life behind them except for repeated, urgent pleas for help.

Such intense demands may seem to indicate a desire for engagement with the other but, in fact, this agitated state is a form of withdrawal. It is an effort to assert an omnipotence of thought in which the words and thoughts of others are cancelled out. Now the individual may turn to thoughts of suicide or retreat into mute, omnipotent rage, predicated on the assumption that, despite all their efforts to ask for help, they have been failed by everyone.

In later chapters I shall be discussing my work with some of these patients in detail. Before that, however, we need to consider the guidelines for working with a person in breakdown. How does one discuss the change of frame?

Chapter 3

The guidelines

The argument of this book is that any relatively experienced psychoanalyst or psychoanalytical psychotherapist should be able to meet the needs of most people who are having a breakdown. However, preparing a person for psychoanalytical work under abnormal circumstances requires close attention to the details of that alteration.

I have already mentioned the need to have a team in place to support the analyst in the clinical task. The analyst is, in effect, providing 'hospital care' in the patient's ordinary environment, without the traumatic effect of hospitalization, and it is vital that, if necessary, the patient be given support to cope with the practical details of life as they become immersed in breakdown.

The analyst's proposal for an extension to the temporal dimensions of the analysis carries serious psychic ramifications. The analyst needs to explain how the frame is changing and why. Rather than trying to explain this in the abstract, I shall quote the following typical approach to this explanation:

> I can see that you are going through a difficult patch and this is an important time for you. It is my standard practice with all my patients when this occurs to propose an increase in the number of sessions in order to give us time to process what is taking place. So, provided you agree, for now I would like you to come every day at your regular hour and

then again at 5.30 p.m. To assist us through this period I would like you to see Dr Branch, a psychiatrist with whom I work, in case we find that you need medication, or any other medical help. I would like you to visit him today or tomorrow, and I can arrange the appointment for you. You will be seeing him once a week, at least for the next few weeks. I would also like you to visit your GP.

If the patient needed further members of an outpatient team then I would say something like:

I think you need some additional support at the moment and I understand that your sister [brother, neighbour, close friend] is aware of your difficulties. If you feel comfortable asking them for daily visits to help you with meals and other things then would you please call them. I cannot have any contact with them because my relationship with you must remain confidential, but please feel free to indicate that this was my recommendation, and do discuss this with your psychiatrist. He may ask to meet with your sister and he will coordinate the care that is required. In my experience this sort of extra help is usually needed for a few weeks at most.

When practising in England I would often add:

In situations of this kind it makes our work easier if your travel to and from the sessions is taken care of. I shall arrange with a local minicab firm to have a driver available to bring you here and take you home. His name is Edward. His fee is very reasonable and he will be unobtrusive and not ask you any questions.

And then, what about fees? I explain this as follows:

Although we are increasing your sessions, you will pay only what you usually pay in the course of a week. This is

> not an exception made for you; it is my usual practice. My
> fee structure takes account of eventualities such as this.

This communication accomplishes several things.

The *way* one puts these changes in the frame to the patient
is crucial. Indicating that these steps are merely standard
practice, indeed, that there has always been a team of people
ready to step in and help out should the need arise, is
enormously reassuring at a time when most analysands are
close to panic.

The explanation functions as a narrative structure that
provides a temporary holding environment, and also prepares
the analysand for what is to come. The repeated use of phrases,
such as 'standard practice' and 'clinical guidelines', underlines
the fact that this is not a personal act of intervention but a
professional one. It emphasizes that the decision is considered,
intelligent, and the best way to proceed. It is simply a
manifestation of one's training. One is implicitly, and
sometimes explicitly, asking the patient to relax and trust the
analytical process.

Gaining the patient's trust in the method and in its
professionalism is extremely important at this point. It is a
crucial moment in the patient's life. If one is able to intensify
the analytic work and set up a holding environment that
meets their needs as they break down, then the experience
can be transformed into a breakthrough that will renew them
for the rest of their lives. If not, it can be a disaster.

In dealing with a person breaking down, above all else,
one does not want to be behind the game. In my experience
of supervising clinicians in these situations, by far the most
common error is that the analyst fails to organize a holding
environment before the breakdown takes hold. Rather than
having anticipated the crisis in order to be there for the
patient as it occurs, they will thereafter be trying in vain to
catch up, responding to something that has already happened.
As the patient has not been held, their panic will increase,
and the originating historical event (or mental structures

organized in early childhood) that are now emerging are met with the same kind of failure, or ego fracture, that occurred in early childhood. The current trauma now becomes an affirmation that the original situation—be it the internalization of parental madness, or the self's own skewed response to the world—is the truth. Once this sets in, I do not think it can be undone.

The tragedy, especially in the United States over the last forty years, is that well-meaning, caring clinicians have been cowed by a fear of litigation into practising a form of defensive psychotherapy. They resort much too readily to referrals to psychopharmacologists, and they fail their patients through their anxiety, hesitation and apparent lack of trust in the psychoanalytic process. I have the greatest respect for my American colleagues, but the impingements on their right to professional freedom are so severe that, too often, they fail to be guided by their clinical judgement in their treatment of very disturbed people. Those who do insist on this, take a courageous risk.

Once the analyst has explained carefully to the analysand that they are guided by their clinical judgement to recommend a change in the treatment plan, analysands will often raise objections.

I regard a certain resistance to this kind of change as a good sign. The desire to sustain normality is part of the life instinct, and it is important for the analyst to support this wish, whilst assuring the patient that the change in intensity is intended merely to help them through the present crisis.

For the most part, all the patients whose analysis was increased to two sessions a day were able to continue in their workplace and needed only minimal time off. In the UK, in contrast to America, people benefit from a fairly flexible workplace idiom that generally allows latitude for people to work, temporarily, for only a few hours a day without provoking intrusive investigation.

From a clinical point of view, it is usually preferable for the person to continue to work, even if they rely for a while on basic procedural memory and habit. I explain that they should not undertake taxing work at this time, and we might discuss what is coming up in the next two weeks, and how certain tasks could be delegated to others for a while. The value of continuing to work is not simply that an important part of their life is undisturbed, it is that the ego functioning intrinsic to work life is sustained. For the method I follow, it is important that *at all times the analyst supports those ego strengths that are present in the analysand,* as they will be an important part of the psychic holding environment and the process of recovery.

Patients will often worry about the fee, and I want to make it clear to the reader that this is not a matter of altruism on my part.

At this point I am concerned for clinical reasons to remove any excess stress from these analysands' lives. Already under great pressure, full of fear, the last thing they need is any anxiety about accruing debt, and I am equally keen to avoid this weighing on my own mind. If I am to manage the task ahead I do not want the burden and distraction of feeling that I have to rush things in case the patient is unable to manage the cost.

By far the easiest solution is to remove the fee as an issue. As I have said, I explain clearly that this my standard practice, and most (non-hysterical) analysands do not experience this as a seductive attempt to make them feel special; at the time they are too traumatized and panicked by their internal state to react in this way. Nonetheless, one must anticipate some retrospective guilt when the recovered patient is contemplating what took place during these regressions. For this reason I always made it clear—occasionally through irony—that my policy is not to charge for the extra sessions, and that I am not going to make an exception for them.

Analysands are often concerned about how they are to explain what is happening to family and friends. However, since those close to the patient are usually already very alarmed by the patient's state, I can point out that the people concerned are likely to be relieved that they are coming for extra sessions in order to tackle the situation.

After clarifying these issues, I introduce the idea of an agreement between the analysand and myself. I request that they adhere to the change in the schedule, and that they undertake to see this through until we both feel that it has been successful. We then go over what I have proposed one last time, and if there are lingering doubts we discuss them. In almost all cases the patient agrees.

There may be a few remaining quibbles: 'But can't I go to dinner with my friends tomorrow?' or 'There is an important new project at work and I really should be in on from the beginning'. I tell them that no, they should not be aiming to do these things at present. The gravity of their condition requires that we take it seriously, and this means that they need to give absolute priority to the treatment. This is a time to seek a form of sanctuary, where psychoanalysis is intensified and where the character of what is happening is allowed its chance to be articulated.

So, before this period of work begins, what is in the minds of the two participants?

The analyst may have some hunches about what will happen when the analysand enters the breakdown with full force but, in my experience, it is best not to second-guess this. An open mind is an unconsciously receptive one. What will be played out in the weeks that follow will, of course, be challenging, but the analyst will be the recipient of precious information from the very heart of his analysand, and now is the time to concentrate deeply, to listen, and to take in everything that is said.

And what is the analysand's understanding of what is about to take place?

Like the high winds and surf that precede a hurricane, there has often been warning enough that something serious is happening and that emergency measures need to be taken. The patient will be experiencing a mixture of signal and primary anxiety, and this will predispose them to form an alliance with the analyst's plan of action as this feels containing. Knowing that there is a psychoanalytic procedure for meeting the intense arrival of mental illness is deeply reassuring.

The estimation of the amount of clinical time to set aside for the patient is a crucial aspect in the fabric of the holding environment. Underestimating the challenge ahead, by offering insufficient sessions at this point, constitutes a fundamental failure, causing the analyst to run the risk of falling behind the pace of the breakdown. If they recommend too many sessions this is much less hazardous as it can be modified without causing damage to the treatment. This must, of course, be a decision that is judged individually in each case but, generally speaking, for a person who is breaking down gradually I have usually recommended additional sessions over an extended period of time, whereas with a patient who has a sudden and acute breakdown I tend to offer all-day sessions.

I do not know how to convey the deep significance of this human-to-human commitment. Over and above the details of the new contract, the analysand understands that a human being is committing themself to seeing them through the worst of what is to come. And that is how I feel. I am prepared to stay with them no matter how long it takes (unless it were to become obvious that my provision was inadequate), and I am sure this conveys itself as part of my communication to the patient.

I need to make it clear that this is not a matter of confidence in my own abilities; it is just that, over the decades, I have become increasingly impressed by the therapeutic efficacy of the psychoanalytical method, giving the person unfettered time to talk freely to the other without fear of judgement. The sincerity and simplicity of this makes profound sense. Human beings are bad at many things, but one of our gifts is the genius of language. Even though much of what takes place in psychoanalysis is non-verbal, the linguistic potential remains *in itself* a reliable thing, a structure that is present in the unconscious, to be used in whatever way it is required.

So, even as the psychoanalyst is asserting their professional standards of practice, the human factor in this extension is already part of the cure. This aspect is particularly powerful if, as is frequently the case, the person who is breaking down lacked adequate human care when they were infants or children. They may have had a mother and father who did the best they could, who performed the duties of parents, went through the motions, were indeed well-intentioned, but when it came down to it, for whatever reasons, just could not bring their humanity into being a good parent. Something of their empathic potential was held in reserve. Maybe the cries of the infant or the needs of the child sent them into remote, defensive parts of their personality for escape, or perhaps they were so distracted by their careers that the child perpetually came second.

But this type of background is not always present in these patients. Childhood is an essentially unfathomable experience, one that cannot be communicated. Even the most attuned parent cannot be witness to the child's internal struggles and sometimes they can be experiencing a profound structural crisis that is simply outside parental perception. In other words, minds are hazardous phenomena and a child's mind is especially vulnerable to the vagaries of life. So whether the child's needs have gone unmet by their parents, or whether they have simply suffered from childhood itself, many selves bring early trauma with them into adult life.

Endemic failure of the childhood self has been usurped in the public and the clinical imagination by scare stories of satanic ritual, sexual molestation or emotional abuse. Crimes against children are common enough to warrant public alarm, and it goes without saying that the victims deserve our clinical attention, but those who have suffered in these overt and violent ways present a different picture to the psychoanalyst from the people described in this text.

We are dealing here with a relatively common situation, one that has been neglected, and it should be of concern even if it lacks the immediacy of the self who has been molested or is psychotic. For when normally functioning people, whom one might diagnose as schizoid, obsessional or depressive, cease to function and collapse into a breakdown, this can destroy their personality potential, their quality of life and relationships, and it can affect their internal world for the remainder of their lives.

Many potentially vulnerable people avoid breakdown by unconsciously providing themselves with curative relationships, or by absorbing themselves in their professional lives. A good partner can sometimes heal the unconscious childhood traumas resident in the adult. Absorption in one's work can be so internally nourishing that, on its own, it can prevent a breakdown that otherwise might have occurred. In adulthood, if the person is fortunate, there may be many single moments which are so unconsciously creative that they serve as psychic genera, healing the self from within; part of the unthought known of everyday life.[1]

This work, then, is about those people who have not found transformative cures for the traumas of childhood, and who are, therefore, fated, at some point in their life, to break down.

Chapter 4

Emily

Emily was in her mid-thirties, and worked at a housing association some ten miles from my consulting room. She had come for analysis, she said, because she felt that although her colleagues saw her as a very competent and helpful person, she believed this was only thanks to a huge effort on her part that kept them unaware of how frightened she felt, and how needy she was. She told me she had been in a long-term relationship with her boyfriend, and it had been very reassuring to have him around, but he had become restless in the last few years and this had increased Emily's anxieties. She looked wan, struggled to speak, and seemed at a loss.

She was referred by her GP for a full analysis. During the first year and a half, she told me a tale of many separations from her parents as a child, her fears of other children and her low academic performance. She was shy, barely looked at me when I greeted her in the waiting room, and went to the couch like someone sleep-walking. She spoke in a very low voice, there were long silences, occasionally she seemed to have difficulty swallowing and often she fought back tears, wiping her eyes with her fingers.

As well as establishing from day-to-day the times when she felt anxious or vulnerable, where she was when she felt this way, and why, I also noted her strengths. Along with a past and a present composed of great pain and personal vulnerability we recognized her abilities: the ways in which she demonstrated skill, resolve and direction in her life.

Without being hostile, she was wary of me. It was as if she could not possibly depend upon me and concluded that she had to keep her distance. We discussed this and all its nuances, connecting her way of being and of relating to fantasies that generated her mentality, and to past events that also influenced her behaviour.

Then one Monday, Emily announced one day that her boyfriend had left her. For some months he had talked of leaving, saying he felt that he could have a better life than the one he was having with her and, on the Sunday, Emily returned from a walk in the park to find their flat empty and a note saying he would be in touch in a few weeks. She fell into her chair and sat there for hours. When I saw her the next day she walked like the living dead. She was white as a sheet, struggled to speak, and there were long silences as she lay on the couch. Her tears flowed. Although the boyfriend's departure was not unexpected, I felt that she would have a hard time surviving this shock.

After her session, with her permission, I telephoned her GP to say that I was concerned with her state and we agreed to keep in touch.

On Tuesday, she came to the session in much the same state but she looked more dishevelled. She said: 'Oh by the way, I just drove my car off the road. It was a write-off.' Although she had felt thrown by this event she had managed to get to work, but it was difficult for her to perform her duties without a car.

On Wednesday, she said nothing at all and was unkempt, as if she had not bathed. I asked whether she was looking after herself. She said 'no', and then was unresponsive. I told her that her collapse made absolute sense to me, that I believed her boyfriend's departure was deeply distressing, but that the feelings connected with it had not arrived yet; she was in shock. I said I thought her car accident, her remoteness in the session, and the fact that she did not appear to me to be eating or looking after herself, indicated that she needed some additional help.

She asked what was I thinking of and I said that it was my standard practice, when someone was in a bad patch, to provide supplementary care, and that I would like be in sustained contact with her GP. At first, she insisted that she was okay, but after a few minutes she broke down into uncontrollable sobbing and said it was all right for me to contact her GP. It was hard for her to get off the couch and leave at the end of the session.

I phoned the GP, we discussed her situation and he agreed to see her the next afternoon.

On Thursday, I told her this. She was unresponsive but before she left I checked again that she had understood about the appointment and she said she would go. I also told her that I wanted to see her at the weekend, to which she agreed, and I said that because she seemed to be feeling disorientated I thought she needed to travel to and from our sessions in a minicab. I informed her that I had a driver I could use for this purpose and that I would arrange for him to collect her from her work, wait outside the consulting room and take her home. Since she was without a car, and as getting around on public transport was now very difficult, she found this helpful. Given her state of mind, we agreed that it would be good to telephone her office and let them know she would not be coming to work the following day.

By Monday, Emily was declining. She had seen her GP and he thought she should probably go into hospital, but we agreed that that we would wait to see how things went in the next few days. With her permission, I arranged for a social worker to visit her early in the evening, to see how she was doing and she seemed relieved by this. When she left the session Edward drove her to work. She found work 'reassuring'. She said that she had managed to put off any difficult tasks, and that her colleagues seemed sympathetic and unintrusive.

She was now having 'visions' that seemed to be eidetic breakthroughs from childhood. They were not hysterical creations; there was no secondary gain, no pleasure from these sightings. They were vivid pictures: her mother in an apron in the kitchen; lying next to her mother's feet as she prepared a meal; the sight of the family car disappearing down the road. The latter related to a period of three years when she was looked after by her aunt, and only saw her parents every few months.

From a psychoanalytical perspective, the material that was emerging was crucial. I listened intently and when I thought I understood how these visions told us something about her past I made interpretations. However, each day when I collected her from the waiting room, Emily seemed more frozen than before and also imbued with a kind of rage. I said this to her in a session, and in the days to come she became deeply angry with me, but she could not fathom why. I said that she did not need to know, or try to speak it—I could see it and feel it—but it seemed to me that I had become the mother/father who had abandoned her, and everything she felt towards them was now coming into the analytical room. Painful as it was, I said, I thought it was essential, in order for her to make contact with the pain and the defences she had used all her life to keep herself afloat.

The social worker reported that there was no food in the house, that Emily had not bathed, and that the house was a mess, with unopened bills, including a tax demand, scattered all over the place. He and his colleagues organized food, got her clothing washed, and helped sort out her flat and her papers.

We met for three weeks, seven days a week, for ninety minutes at a time. Then, for the next two months, we returned to five days a week, but still with ninety-minute sessions. Within three months Emily had come through her breakdown.

Throughout those weeks, with the exception of only a few days, she had gone to work. The visions of her mother during her early childhood released previously bound affect and she survived the mental pain of this reliving. Her body bearing shifted: whereas before she had always walked stiffly, she now seemed more filled out and she moved more freely in space, as if she were communicating a more human dimension.

For the next two years, however, Emily was still in considerable mental pain, and the realization of her early losses continued to appear in session after session. She had always had an intellectual grasp of her childhood deprivations and she knew that her sense of unreality as an adult was owing to the fact that she had withheld herself from life because she did not trust it. But now she knew directly, through the emotional experience, why she had lived the way she had for all that time.

A crucial aspect of the process of transformation for people in breakdown is the alliance with the healthy parts of the person's self, as these will become the scaffolding upon which a new self will emerge. In Emily's case, this alliance was used effectively. Our acknowledgement of her ego assets—the part of her self that got her to work—now enabled her to use them to move forward in her life, endowed with a new emotional presence.

In a sense, breakdown and recovery mirror the normal process of growth and development. We begin life in an infantile state and we have parents upon whom we depend and who care for us, but from the start we also have a core self that is developing. Both forms of provision—externally from the parents and internally from the growing ego—are essential to the self's development.

Although I had set up a team to receive Emily's breakdown and I felt that we were ready, I realized afterwards that I had been too cautious. When the social worker reported the state of her living conditions it was clear that she was in very dire straits and that she should have been reached earlier. I allowed her to suffer for too long before taking action and, ironically, it was partly my anxiety about committing what I feared might be an analytical transgression that prevented me from acting earlier.

Undoubtedly, I was also anxious about the task I faced. If the countertransference is too agitated the analyst will not be able to manage the clinical requirements that present themselves. Above all, they need to be in that meditative position that Freud advocated so brilliantly. They will have to find their way to 'evenly suspended attentiveness', in order to receive the analysand's free associations and character presentations.

The new frame is set in place in order, first, to look after the analyst so that they can be settled enough in their mind to be able to think and to be of help to their patients. When I was working with I Emily, I hardly knew her GP, I had met Edward only once, and I was not yet sufficiently familiar with the social work team to know for sure that the back-up system would work. I was not being securely held.

I realized that the slowness of my response to Emily's deterioration meant a prolongation of her distress. What might have taken only two weeks, had I been better prepared, lasted for several months. The mental pain she endured was due in part, to my failure to secure the holding environment in time, thus recreating aspects of her early childhood.

From this time forward I was determined, should I be presented with a similar situation, that I would move much more quickly to initiate intensive analysis, and to establish an effective care system.

Chapter 5

Anna

For several years, Anna, in her mid-forties, had been coming to see me for psychotherapy. A vibrant, upbeat, brilliant woman, she managed a leading IT firm in London. She lived alone but had many friends and lovers. Although she was not ideologically opposed to marriage or monogamy she wasn't eager to get into a long-term relationship.

One Thursday, when she arrived at 3 p.m. for her session, I could hardly believe what I saw. Normally beautifully kitted out, rosy-cheeked and facially expressive, she was dishevelled, ashen-faced and without expression. She sat in the chair, smiled wanly and, as usual, began with an introductory comment:

'Well, let's see … what I can talk about today?'

'What's wrong?'

'What do you mean?'

'You look awful.'

'I do?'

'You don't know that?'

'No. Well, I don't exactly feel brilliant …'

'I have never seen you look this devastated before.'

'Ah. Well …' (She was silent).

'Yes?'

'Something happened. It shouldn't bother me so much. I didn't know it showed, so I'm surprised you picked up on it, but it's a small matter.'

As Anna spoke her mouth dried up and I fetched a glass of water and put it next to her on a side table. She gulped it down, tried to talk and then froze completely. For the next ten minutes she stared at me in silence. She kept trying to speak, putting her hand over her mouth, looking up at the ceiling and pushing her hands together as though trying to force herself into speech. I said it was okay, she should take her time. I left the room, refilled her glass of water, and put a note on my external door stating that owing to unforeseen circumstances I would not be able to keep appointments that day. I knew that Anna was having a breakdown.

After about half an hour she tried again to talk, but she was not coherent, and this clearly raised her level of anxiety. I said that it was fine, that whatever it was that had upset her she would have enough time to tell me about it, and that she should just rest until she could get to that point. She nodded, tears ran down her cheeks, and she stared at me, at the ceiling, around the room, fixing her eyes on different objects, then back to tears, more silence, and me.

After about forty minutes she whispered, 'Christopher, I have to go. My time is nearly up.' She looked down to her left to find her bag, which she had actually put behind her chair. I said that I had put a notice on my door saying that I would not be able to meet with other patients that day, and that we would continue until 6 p.m., so that she should relax. She tried to protest but couldn't summon the energy to do so and slumped back in her chair. I left the room for a few minutes and left messages on my patients' answer machines, cancelling their sessions that day, and when I returned I gave her another glass of water.

After two hours or so she was able to speak, but in a way that was unprecedented for her. In place of her customary cheeriness, she spoke slowly, in a low voice and with a false calm. She told me how Griselda, a close friend of hers of many years, had told her the day before that she thought that Anna was 'a self-centred bitch' and that she wasn't sure she wanted to continue the relationship. Anna paused, bit her lip, and then said that this had been such a 'stunning' statement that she could not believe it.

One theme of the analysis up until that point had been how Anna thrived on the love of many people. She was immensely popular and she handled minor everyday disputes, in her workplace, for example, without much difficulty. She was, however, given to unconscious self-idealization and her friend's comment had shattered her sense of self. The person sitting in front of me now was in a new and terrible internal place; she seemed completely empty of herself and without resources.

There are some vital elements that the analyst has to have in place in order to help someone through a breakdown, and one is a clear understanding of the *line of conflict* in the person's history. When a breakdown comes, one of the fundamental factors in finding a way through it is the psychoanalyst's clear explanation of what is happening and why.

To Anna I said:

'All your life you have had to believe you were perfect and you have been loved by everyone, because if you weren't wonderful, you felt you were nothing. Hating your mother as you did, you rescued yourself by idealizing your father. He idealized you, and by adolescence you could feel that you were a wonderful person. You had to be, in order to conceal the part of you that could hate someone so violently that you would lose your sense of self.'

The most important feature of the containing environment in psychoanalysis is the act of interpretation. Each interpretive step is part of 'psychoanalytical holding'. People feel understood, not simply through the presence of an empathic other but, more importantly, through the intelligent grasp the analyst has of why this person is in the fix they are in. Indeed, at this level, interpretation is a form of love. Being known is being loved at a crucial time in one's life.

As I made this interpretation to Anna I spoke slowly and calmly. I conveyed to her that, of course, this was bound to happen at some point and, although painful, it was not odd.

This communication is essential because when someone starts to breakdown they have to deal, not only with the traumatic issue that set off the breakdown, but also with a secondary panic over the fact that they are having a breakdown. It is this primary anxiety that is the most toxic, and it needs immediate attention. It is important to convey to the person that their worry is understandable and that they are going to be okay.

Telling someone that they are going to be okay may seem unremarkable at an ordinary social level, but it violates the laws imposed by psychoanalysis. Received wisdom is that psychoanalysts are not meant to say something like this. And I would agree that we should *never* say this unless we believe it. We cannot provide forecasts for any patient's future based on conjectures or probabilities. When we speak to our analysands we are obliged to speak the truth, and if we sometimes withhold a comment, thereby perhaps committing an untruth by omission, it is in the interests of tact, not of deception.

When I said to Anna that what was happening was understandable and that she would be okay, I deeply believed this to be so. With the team supporting me, and bearing in mind that I was willing to work from dawn till dusk, for as long as it took to help her through her breakdown, I was simply convinced that the psychoanalytical process was so efficient, so inherently transformative, that it would do the work. I have no doubt that I convey this trust to patients, and that my belief in the life instincts (the developmental process) plays an important role in mitigating their panic.

I told Anna that she was having a breakdown and that we had work to do and steps to take. I said that I had seen people through this before, it was part of my profession to work with people in such circumstances, but if we were going to get through this she would have to cooperate with my guidelines.

I said that she would have to set aside all duties for the following day (Friday) and that I would work with her from 9 a.m. to 6 p.m. I said that before she left I would arrange an appointment for her that evening with Dr Branch, who she had seen before. They would meet, then she should go home, have some dinner, stay off the phone, and go to sleep. I contacted Dr Branch and he was ready to see her. He, in turn, telephoned Edward to arrange for her to be collected from my office at 6 p.m.

By telling her we would stop at a specific time I was accomplishing two things. I was affirming that this was a *boundaried* meeting, that it had a time frame. This time-sense is very important for the self's ego and forms part of its route to recovery. The fear of infinity is an immediate consequence of the onset of any breakdown and so, as one increases the length of the sessional time, it must be mitigated by a frame that is adhered to. If one said, 'Don't worry, we can stay here until you are ready to leave', this would abandon the patient to their own ego functioning, which would simply create more panic.

This was not, however, simply a therapeutic device. My bargain with myself was simple: if the patient was unable to leave at the prescribed time then this indicated that it would not be possible to see this person through a breakdown, and I would be obliged to send them to hospital. So the new frame also represented the boundary of my approach.

By using numbers—'we will stop at six' rather than 'we will stop in two hours'—I employed the symbolic order. This served as an anchor point in the process of therapeutic transformation. Whatever was to happen between nine and six—and I knew that all hell would break loose—these numbers stood both for the limitation of the time to be spent together and for the time allotted to the unconscious to have its breakdown. I had learned that people who are in this state have an unconscious sense of how to use what is provided, as long as the analyst, as the guardian of the space and time, adheres to the frame.

Anna said, 'But, Christopher … I can't go and see Dr Branch. I have a crucial international telephone conference this evening. I can't miss it. I have to do this.' She was highly driven, professionally, and it was not at all unusual for her to work a fifteen-hour day, six days a week. At this point, as I have said, the patient's resistance to the change of parameters is good sign. It demonstrates a reluctance to having life disrupted, as if the ego is saying, 'I am not going to succumb to this. I can get through it myself. Thanks for your concerns but I will be fine.' Ultimately, those inner resources will be crucial to the self's recovery, to its return to ordinary life, and to the transformative potential of the breakdown.

It is important, therefore, for the analyst to confirm the validity of those resistances.

'Look Anna, I know this is important and I respect your wish to do it, and you will have your conferences in a few days' time, but not just now.'

When she protested again, I said, 'You are in no shape for it. The world will be okay without you for a few days, and I can't help you through this unless you get on board.'

This is the moment when analyst and patient negotiate the terms of the treatment during breakdown. This contract is vital. Having validated and empathized with the patient's resistance to the proposed change in practice, the next step is to gain full cooperation with the new treatment plan. No two plans are the same: there will be variations in what to do, for how long, who is to be involved, and so forth.

Anna lived alone, but she had a next-door neighbour who was a very good, caring friend, and I knew that this would be the best person to keep an eye on her. The neighbour knew she was in analysis with me and, as my protocol is not to talk with friends or members of the family except in very exceptional circumstances, I asked Anna if she would kindly call her friend and ask her to come round that night for half an hour or so. She should tell her that she was going through a bad patch, and ask that she drop in on her over the next few days. Anna agreed to this, and indeed her friend proved to be a crucial assistant during the following week.

Six o'clock came round. Her comportment had not changed. She still looked terrible and was barely coherent, but she managed a smile and said, 'Christopher, you sure are one tough character'.

I knew that she was referring to my negotiating stance, my insistence upon reaching a plan of action, which had demonstrated an aspect of my personality that would probably not have been evident under ordinary analytical circumstances. This moment involves a combination of maternal care and paternal structure. The analyst has to balance the provision of a holding environment that will allow for, and contain, deep regression but they must, at the same time, bring paternal, structuring elements to bear on the patient's recuperation.

Edward was at the door to take Anna to Dr Branch's office for her appointment. Edward's contribution during the next few days was another important part of her being 'in care' at all times, even when she was alone. The journey from where I practised to Dr Branch was a twenty-minute drive, and I wanted Anna to be with someone who would know how to respond: when to talk, and when to leave her to be quiet.

Later, I talked with Dr Branch and he confirmed that this was a depressive breakdown and that Anna was very close to not coping.

However, I was in a fix. I was supposed to leave the next day for New York and then go on to Austen Riggs for a week's visit, lecturing, supervising and giving a public lecture.[1] I wrote to the director, Gerrard Fromm, and told him that, to my great regret, I could not come because I had a patient who was in breakdown. The next morning I received an email that was characteristic, not only of him but of the whole ethos of the Riggs community. He said that I was right to do this and that they supported me in my approach, and he asked that I keep them posted as to her progress.

In those days, Riggs had a daily morning conference when the nurses, analysts, and staff would meet and go over what had happened during the night. Plastic coffee cups dotted the table as people woke up once again to the reality that they were looking after borderline or psychotic patients, and the gallows humour of the staff helped everyone through the anxieties of the report.

It is a measure of Riggs' empathy that they knew what I was going through in London, and what it meant for me to have to cancel my visit. Each day I would send a brief message letting them know how my patient was, and this would be included in the daily meeting, just as if my patient and I were part of the community there. I was very moved by this and it was an important part of my own holding environment.

The following morning Edward delivered Anna to my consulting room and we began at nine. As with all the patients presented here, it is not possible, for reasons of confidentiality, to provide as many details I would like, so the following is a brief summary.

For some hours Anna found it hard to talk. I had supplied bottles of water next to her chair and she drank one after the other.[2] Every so often she tried to speak, then slumped back in her chair, spreading her legs, hands clenched between them, as if she was trying to find her body first, before words could come. Every so often I would say, 'Take your time, there's no rush', and she would relax back in her chair and look off into space. Then the word 'Right!' shot out of her mouth and she began describing in much more detail what her friend had said, where she had said it, and why it was so disturbing. She looked at me, tears streaming down her face:

'How can people be so terrible? How could such a loyal friend be such a, such a ...'

'Shit?'

'Yes, how could she be such a shit?'

'Well, I don't know. I don't know Griselda. You have so many friends it is hard to keep track.'

'I have never given her cause to be angry with me, or to say that.'

'Perhaps, but you are the sort of centre of a remarkable community of people who adore you.'

'What does that mean?'

'People love you; you love the fact that they love you. I expect Griselda was pissed off.'

'Oh, come on, I mean, I never gave her cause to say something like that to me. Never. I never did.'

'So perhaps it was her only way to get through to you.'

'I am not difficult to get through to! I think I am open to what anyone says! [pause] Christopher, do you find me difficult to get through to?'

'Yes, I do.'

'You *do?*'

'Yes, you are so bubbly and full of yourself I haven't a clue what goes on inside you when you are down, when things aren't just great.'

'Well, fuck you!'

'Um.'

'Well … I mean … Really? You don't? What do you mean "when I'm down?" What are you talking about?'

'Anna, you can be unreal. You are trying to get through life as if it's all just one happy camp-out. And you can do it by keeping your distance from people, just as you keep distance from me. You are terrific, strong, brilliant; you have a lot that is healthy in you. But … you can be false.'

'I don't know about that. I don't know … I mean …'

At this point she tapered off, stopped talking for a while, drank from another bottle of water, got up to go the lavatory, came back, sat down, and then started sobbing. The crying went on slowly and rhythmically for an hour or more, then it stopped. It was 12.30 p.m., time for our lunch break, and I said I would see her at 1.15 p.m. There was a café around the corner where she could get a sandwich and she returned on time.

Breaks are very important; whether for a weekend, a holiday or even an hour, the break creates a change of place and this brings a new perspective. The patient needs to be away from the other in order to think differently.

Anna had been mulling me over and transforming what I said into her own musings. For an hour she said nothing, but she was less depressed and seemed thoughtful.

'Okay. I get it. I think you are right about my being unreal. I know about it. I think I have always *known* about it, Christopher, but I just did not know what to *do* about it. It always seemed to work. It kept peace at home, it made my father happy, it kept me away from my mother's throat, and I had great sex with fantastic men for ten years. Life was great and I have done well, but ...'

'You keep moving, on the run, so that you don't have a chance to think about yourself.'

'Well, who would want to? [she laughed] I mean, okay, you are right, but I am not so sure that relationships work really ... and I know I am alone, but this is fine by me.'

It was as if Anna had been punched in the back. She coughed and leaned forward, then righted herself, looked straight at me, smiled, broke down in tears and sobbed. After ten minutes she said:

'Oh shit, Christopher, *what* am I going to do?'

'You are doing it.'

'I am in such trouble.'

'A bit of trouble.'

'What! A *bit* of trouble?'

'I've seen a lot worse.'

'Oh great, well lucky you! '

She was quiet for fifteen minutes, drank more water, and then there was a long narrative about her mother, her childhood and her young adulthood.

At 5.55 p.m. I let her know that we would end in five minutes. Edward picked her up and took her home. She telephoned Dr Branch, as arranged, had a meal with her neighbour and fell into bed exhausted, sleeping through the night.

The session had gone well. Anna knew that she had disintegrated, that her old self was finished and that a new one would emerge. Or, put another way, the false self, derived from defences against her childhood hatred toward her mother, had collapsed and something more true to herself was now emerging. Although there were worrying times in the session—when she spaced out, appeared to be vacating herself—she had always come back.

My comments were often confronting and to the point, because conversational idiom often seems intuitively correct at moments such as these. One side effect of brevity and frankness is that it is digestible (a kind of psychic sound bite) and, if it is given with affection, it rouses affect in the analysand, and mobilizes generative aggression.[3] This aggression is part of the essential play of being human. It is not fluffy, idealized, *Sesame Street* play, but the play of wit and truth: a play that gets to the heart of things. Like the joke, this kind of play is an emotional experience, condensing many of the self's unconscious preoccupations in its brevity.

Such play takes place ego-to-ego. My comments, her comments, were part of an ongoing mobility of thought that was gathering her affect, again and again. Even as she was descending into the depths of her depression she was, simultaneously, building the new self that would arise out of this experience. Of course she did not know this, but I had, by this time, witnessed this feature—the presence of recovery in the midst of breakdown—many times and could feel at ease with it.

On Sunday Anna arrived at 9 a.m. She was distressed.

'Christopher, I shat myself.'

'Right.'

'I … I … was in bed this morning, and without thinking, or even knowing, suddenly there was a flood of shit everywhere and I was covered in it.'

'Disturbing.'

'*That's* an understatement. I didn't believe it at first, but then I did. So I got up, went into the shower, got all the shit off me, then went back into the bedroom gathered up all the sheets, put them in the laundry, and … well …'

'So you took care of it.'

'Yes, but I shat myself. That means something. It means that I am in *real* trouble.'

'Anna, I think it was a good thing.'

'What?'

'You have been *too* self-controlled, keeping all your shit in. So you had a good rest, you were calm, and you were free enough to let some of the shit out.'

'Are you kidding?'

'Of course not.'

'But I can't go around shitting myself like that!'

'Actually Anna, I think it would be a good thing if you had a little more shit on yourself than you do.'

At this point Anna roared with laughter and continued to chuckle for the next ten minutes.

'Right, so I get it. This process is one in which I am supposed to come out of here having felt like shit, then get covered in it, which is a good thing, right?'

'I have to think about that.'

'I've stumped you.'

'Yes.'

'Well *good* for me!'

Time passed, then I said:

'I think what you were saying is quite profound really. I *do* think if you can be less squeaky clean and more real, perhaps revealing that you are a bit of a shit, that you have shitty thoughts, then you won't force friends like Griselda to have to punch you because you are so offensively goody goody.'

Anna went silent. She looked to the left and then around the room, in a pose I had seen before which meant, 'I am really thinking about this one'. Then, after ten minutes:

'I think I get this. My Zeitgeist is not working. I can't fool people into thinking I am so wonderful when I know I'm not. They know I'm not, and so I have to get real. I get it. So, how much longer do you think I have to stay here? I mean, I think I get it, and so I can go now, or in an hour or so, right?'

'You know, Anna, you have just shown us something: how you are a kind of quick study artist. You have grasped a point, but now you are using it to get out of here and escape from that point; to reduce it to an intellectual insight.'

'Oh shit!'

'Right.'

'So, you don't buy what I said?

'No, I believe you. But I think you are exploiting your mind in order to avoid the emotional experience that is resident in the insight you have just reached.'

'What do you mean?'

'I think you are trying to get out of this room as fast as you can. With the first sense of recovery, which I do think is happening, you are going to rush out of here like you rushed out of your family; escaping before you really had to go through the process of working through the shit going on in your mind, in your family.'

'Christ, you know, sometimes I could just kill you. You are so fucking bright. It's so upsetting.'

'Anna, it's not that I'm bright. What you have just done here and now is obvious. It's what your friends see, and remember ... you elected to show it to me. So it's down to your own honesty really.'

There was silence for an hour or so. This moment is hard to convey but it was transformative. Anna had gained insight, but she had used her intellect to try to flee and I had confronted her. In pointing out that it was her own disclosure of this, rather than my cleverness, that had discerned this fact, I had sided with the part of her that really did want to work on herself, that did not want to escape into a false and manic solution to her problems.

Anna met with me for three days from nine to six. At the end of the third day she had recovered from the core of her breakdown and I told her that, for the next two weeks, I wanted to see her daily, including Saturdays, for forty-five-minutes a session. I gave her an end date. I had by then consulted with Dr Branch, Anna had given me her neighbour's assessment ('I think you are coming through this, Anna') and the time frame seemed to be ego-appropriate.

Two weeks later we resumed her ordinary session times.

Anna's breakdown was inevitable. Indeed, I think it was only her remarkable strength that had prevented it from occurring earlier. It took place in the way it did because she was in psychotherapy and because of a convergence of events: one of which, incidentally, had been the prospect of my departure for a week. We both learnt much from this, but it is what the patient learns about themself that is transformative. The learning that takes place within the self's breakdown is deep emotional learning. It is thought saturated in the self's truth, and my experience is that as long as the psychoanalyst sticks with the person through this transition, it will work.

With Emily and Anna, the onset of their breakdowns was sudden and derived from an immediate traumatic encounter. It both cases, however, I was aware of basic faults existing within their personalities and, although we cannot know how they would have fared had they not been clobbered by reality, I reckoned that it would only have been a matter of time before they ground to a halt and became helpless. The structure of the analysis—in the form of interpretations of their lives, and transference to myself—constituted a matrix that was in place before the crisis, and it is these ordinary aspects of analysis that are crucial in work with people in breakdown.

Chapter 6

Mark

Mark was a well-known painter; highly successful, reclusive, but socially adroit and charming when the occasion demanded. He came to analysis in his mid-life because he had never been in love, and he agreed with his friends who said that he was aloof and unknowable. Although he loved painting, even that was starting to feel more like a commercial production than a creative act.

He took to free association, was a highly productive analysand and, in the first two years of analysis, gained new insights into himself, began dating and learned from his failures in relational encounters. Transferentially, he maintained a neutral distance from me, although now and then when he was travelling he would write letters of warmth, affection and appreciation.

Then, through life circumstances, he had to leave London and move to Seattle, and he asked if we could continue analysis by phone. In those days I was sceptical about this, but I agreed on a trial basis to see if it would work. We agreed dates when he would travel to London and we could meet in person, and it so happened I also taught seminars in Seattle, where I was used to renting a suite in which to teach, so I would be able to see him there as well.

Two years on, Mark had continued to make positive changes. Most importantly, he had fallen in love for the first time in his life, and we had understood why this had not been possible until then. His mother had been depressed in his first four years, and when he was twelve he had to cope with the death of his father, from whom he was estranged. At that point Mark froze himself, and decided that he would never give his affections to anyone. He was decent to his mother, but he felt a deep and unmoveable rage against her for failing him in his early life. He believed that only through an almost fanatical independence had he become a success in his career. When women fell in love with him—as they did rather frequently—he immediately resented them because he felt as if they were trying to interfere with his loyalty to himself. He would fail to attend the openings of his exhibitions, retreating into his house, feeling that people were 'cashing in' on his success, and that were he not so good at what he did he would be of no interest to anyone.

So when Mark fell in love with Joyce he was in completely new territory. It was a tumultuous relationship. She was fifteen years his junior, also an artist, sexually gifted, exotic. And she shared his habit; just as he would disappear, so too would she. This mirroring of himself, a part of Joyce's own character, disarmed Mark, but it also created a desperate anxiety in him. Analysis of the fact that he projected into her his vengeful hatred toward his mother helped him to gain some perspective on his reaction to her disappearances, understanding that they were her attempt to recover from her fears of dependence upon him. But he suffered deeply.

After a year of living together they both regressed. Joyce became manic and violent, throwing things at him and screaming at him in public places, and he would respond by going into a cultivated place of hurt, which he knew well and had used against his parents. But increasingly this failed to work. Out of the blue he flew into rages and, on one occasion, he broke up most of the furniture in their flat, then collapsed into a foetal position for a few hours after which he fled the apartment.

Then Mark discovered to his horror that Joyce was a thief. Not a casual amateur, but a semi-pro. He happened upon her stash of stolen jewellery and when he confronted her she said that of course she had stolen them, from parties they had attended. How else was she to finance her career? He might be a success but she was not, and she needed the money.

Mark decided to break off the relationship and he called upon ancient styles of rejection within him. He knew how to put someone in the deep freeze, having done this to his parents many times, but it was clear this was not working. He still loved Joyce. As we talked on the phone, there were long pauses during which I felt, not a remove, but thickening helplessness. During one Wednesday session it was clear that Mark was breaking down and I said I would see him the next day at 4 p.m. I managed to get a flight to Seattle and met him the next day at the hotel.

It was striking that Mark had offered no resistance to my statement that I would see him the next day, but when we met it was not difficult to see why. When I waved at him in the foyer of the hotel he did not move. I went up to him and said, 'Come this way' and he followed me like a zombie.

We talked from 4 to 6 p.m. I said that we would work each day from 9 a.m. to 6 p.m. with an hour for lunch; that I did not know how long it would take to see him through his crisis, but that this should not be of concern. We went over the ground rules. I said I did not want him driving to the sessions and asked that he arrange to travel by taxi. I said that I thought that he was inside a breakdown—he nodded—and I said that we would have some difficult days ahead but I was confident that, if he could stick with it, we would be okay. I had contacted a local psychiatrist/psychoanalyst that I knew from my seminars, and he agreed that he would by on standby should I need him. I knew of a local hospital that I could use and the hotel had a good cab company.

The next morning Mark arrived on time at 9 a.m. He seemed calmer and was tastefully attired. We arrived in the consulting room suite, he saw the bottles of water lined up and said, 'Thanks, that's nice'. He lay on the couch and I sat behind him. He said nothing for the first fifteen minutes but drank several times from a bottle of water. Each time he would screw the top back on very carefully, looking at it with great concentration as he did so.

'Well!' He laughed, then said 'So, where do I begin?'

But the words were hardly out of his mouth before he turned on his side, faced the wall and uttered an indescribable cry. It was a kind of bursting sound that gave rise to intense sobbing that went on for two hours. On occasion he would stop for a moment, sometimes he would drink water, once or twice he went to the lavatory, then he would come back to the couch, turning to the wall, and the sobbing would return. He was unable to speak and I said nothing.

Later, when he did start to talk, his voice was hoarse and seemed clogged with affect. 'Why?' he repeated again and again over the next five minutes. 'I love her. Why did she do this?' Although he was speaking out loud, these were not questions directed at me for an answer and I remained quiet. Noon came around very quickly, he went to eat for an hour and we resumed at one.

The remainder of the day was much the same. His comments continued to be fundamentally rhetorical, and I have found this to be an essential function in self-recovery. The person has first to hear their own thoughts, to have them echo in the psychoanalytical space well before the analyst begins to comment. This forms part of a transition from reaction to the present crisis to the underlying trauma that it has activated. The primary link will be made by the analysand's affect, and after this what the analyst says will have an entirely different meaning.

Around 4 p.m. Mark became more pensive. He had sobbed for most of the day, had drunk seven small bottles of water, and had often tossed and turned on the couch, although there were also long periods of time when he was still but not asleep. He then said in a calm voice that it was so strange; he had had to reject her, he did not wish to, and *he* was the one who felt abandoned.

'I think that's so odd, because in the past I wouldn't let anyone get close to me, or I would slam the door in their face and it felt gratifying. I wanted to hurt them. I didn't want to hurt Joyce. I love her. I had to do it, but I am not sure I can survive it.'

'I think if your one-year-old self could speak about having to reject your mother because of her depression and her coldness, this is what he would say.'

'That I had to reject her and yet I felt abandoned?'

'Yes, I think so.'

'It feels so right what you say. My mother was not a bad woman, she …'

At this point he went silent and then sobbed for another hour. It was the first time in all the years I had known him that he had expressed any feeling at all towards his mother, and now he was deeply inside deferred grief.

Six o'clock came too soon, I felt. I let him know about five minutes before we stopped. I said that I would prefer he just go home, have a bite to eat and get an early night, and that I would see him the next morning at 9 a.m. He said nothing and left the room with his shoulders hunched, looking drained.

He arrived on time the next morning and told me that within ten minutes of eating a small meal, he had gone to bed and slept for twelve hours. I knew from experience that this was a very common outcome of a day-long session. The patient is exhausted by the analysis and usually sleeps through the night.

He apologized and said he had nothing on his mind. There was about half an hour's silence, he drank from a bottle of water, then he went to the lavatory, returned and seemed calm.

'I am thinking about my rejection becoming my abandonment. I think I have been practising that all my life. Correction. I think I practised it as a child for quite some time until it became second nature. Except then I found pleasure in doing it, no longer feeling that I was abandoned

but that other people had to experience *my* abandonment. I
did that a lot to my mother and my father.'

'It makes sense, doesn't it?'

'Because I got a kick out of it?'

'Because you transformed a situation where you were
helpless into one where you were in charge.'

'Man, that explains a lot.'

He was silent for an hour. Our brief exchange is typical of
this kind of work. This was the moment when he was ready
to understand how his character had become structured
around a defence against the emotional experience of
abandonment. When a patient comes to this kind of insight
my custom is to help them to see how their childhood
defences make sense.

I have also learned that in breakdown patients can take
only so much interpretation, after which they need long
periods of silence. These are not introjective moments; I do
not think they are fundamentally taking something in from
the analyst. Rather, I think something known but not thought
(the unthought known) is released by the analyst's comment.
It is very important, therefore, for the analyst to disappear as
an interpretive presence, to allow the patient time for the full
course of the unthought known to arrive, through memories,
emotional experiences and free associations.

Lunch came, and we resumed at one.

Mark was quiet for some time and then he talked about
Joyce.

'I think I picked her because I could love her. In the break
a question crossed my mind. "Why did I love her so much?"
And I know it is because I could feel her vulnerability, I could
see her struggling against something impervious and I loved
her for it.'

'You could see her struggling against yourself.'

'My coldness.'

'Yes.'

'And she survived me and she kept on trying and never
gave up.'

A new round of sobbing followed this statement, then after about fifteen minutes he carried on talking:

'I loved her but she was destroying me. It was too much.'

'I think you tried again and again, as a small boy, to get through to your mother and father. And then it felt as if it was destroying you and you gave up. Joyce is the first person with whom you have shared this experience, and she was your proxy in some ways.'

'She was in my place.

'Yes, I think so.'

'I think I know so. The worst moments were when I realized I was beginning to ... to ... ah ...'

'Hate her?'

'Yes, to hate her. I thought that it was good. It seemed to help. I think I wanted it to continue.'

'As always, it would make things easier.'

'Yes, and ... but ...'

'It wasn't working, because you loved her.'

Mark cried for a long time. Then for a couple of hours he was quiet and seemed pensive. He got up twice to go to the lavatory, then cracked open a new bottle of water and drank it down. Of course he knew I was in the room, but he was off in a world all of his own and there seemed no need to acknowledge me or make customary social gestures. I was reminded of my kids when they were in their cots, just looking around and quite content.

After a long time he said he thought he was okay. He discussed why he knew he had to leave Joyce and he listed the reasons why her immaturity and impetuosity were simply too crazy-making. He said he had learned now that he could love and that he could be in a relationship, and he turned to a theme I had enunciated many times in the analysis: that I had seen him taking progressive steps toward finding the right partner for himself. He said he now believed I was correct. He was no longer going to fuck around with just any woman; he would find someone who was right for him.

His voice and demeanour had changed. He had emerged from his breakdown. He had let me know that on the previous two nights he had been more exhausted than ever before and had slept deeply, feeling cured by sleep itself. Around four in the afternoon he fidgeted, and I said that I thought he had come through his breakdown and that the feeling in the room was different.

'Until about half an hour ago I had no sense of time in here. I only ever got up to go to the lavatory. When you first told me it was time for lunch it felt as if I'd been in the room for only a few minutes and the day flew by. I never thought I was going to recover from the loss of Joyce, so I'm rather amazed at how I could have done so.'

'We gave you time.'

'Well, yes, that's true. I was panicked last week. I had terrible nightmares and an unbearable sense of loss. I thought I could not survive it.'

'Well, you certainly have expressed your loss of her here and that has honoured your feelings for her.'

'Yes, it's a curious way to put it, but apt. I tried very hard with her and she could not stick it out. I hope she's going to be okay.'

He then talked about Joyce and how he could help her in the months to come. She was not well off, and he considered how he could assist her financially whilst retaining his distance from her.

With an hour or so to go I said that I thought we had accomplished our task and that we would resume the analysis on the phone in two days' time. Mark said that was fine. At six he got up, we shook hands, he said, 'Thank you very much', and I said 'It's part of my job'. He walked out of the door and I packed my suitcase and went to the airport.

Chapter 7

Histories and the *après-coup*

In previous essays I have distinguished between past and history.[1] The past is the raw lived experience of our self as we exist as a thing amongst other things. But the facts of our life mean little unless and until they are subjected to unconscious transformation. No act we commit, no act committed against us, no event in our past means anything unless we give it meaning. We all have a past, but not all of us have a history.

Some people have thought a lot about their past; they have created 'histories'. In psychoanalysis, those histories are important as they reflect the work of transforming past experience from a thing into the imaginary and symbolic orders that generate meaning. However, these histories may be replete with self-deceptions aimed often, but not always, at averting the gaze from painful elements of the past. Part of the work of psychoanalysis then, is to reconstruct the self's many histories into the revised, co-constructed version that is the product of analysis.

Bearing in mind that we only ever understand a small part of our mind, it is fortunate that the act of historicity seems to elicit information from the unconscious. One of the functions of the unconscious is to store the disturbing experiences of the child-self for a time in the future when it will be transformed into narrative and consciousness. It is as though the impact of the real is retained unconsciously and given psychic priority, so that if we become historians of the self, at a later time in our life, these areas are sent to us marked 'special delivery'. Certainly the presence of the analyst, who not only announces an interest in the past but takes a meticulous record of recent events and then relates them to ancient history, affects the analysand's unconscious and opens the door to primary source material being released from the libraries of the unconscious.

The history put together when a person is in breakdown is usually very clear. It is simple to explain to them why they are in crisis. A breakdown is a paradoxical gestalt: a moment of self-fragmentation is, at the same time, a moment of coming together inside the self. In the end, it is formative more than it is fracturing. However, because the form of the self's truth is now asserting itself, the strategies employed formerly to deter, defer and avoid it at all costs, now start to crumble, and this alarms the ego, whose aim is to defend the self against endopsychic danger.

This is one of those moments in which the interests of the ego and those of the self are at odds. For the self, a truth is beginning to emerge in the form of an existential crisis embedded with latent meaning. For the ego, the irruption is experienced as a threat to defences long set in place against the inevitable force of that truth ever emerging.

In the moment of breakdown two pasts meet: the immediate past of the event that constitutes the onset; and the patient's childhood. The dream-like condensation of the critical event that has the self reeling, requires free associative deconstruction and emotional saturation before its story can be told. As this work is being done, the recent experience notifies the many stages in the self's past that now is the time for freedom of information, and connecting links are made between recent past and childhood.

One might expect this discovery to be revelatory, but in fact I have not found this to be the case. Although the meeting of the two pasts is profound and moving, the content is not usually a matter of surprise.

Mark set up defences against allowing people to get inside him because he had a mother who was paranoid. He knows he does this. Then he falls in love, allows his lover to get close to him, she walks off and he breaks down. On the face of it the reasons for the collapse seem fairly obvious but, intriguingly, although such explanations may not be new, as analyst and patient articulate these simple understandings within the new situation, most analysands find the past presenting itself in a new form; one in which it is restated or narrated differently. It seems that it is not the content of the past which is therapeutic at this point, but the *act of history-making* that is generative and transformative.

So what is the nature of the deferred experience that eventually arrives to cause a breakdown?

In an earlier work, I argued that a child that is inside a disturbing psychological event will freeze-frame it.[2] This unconscious activity aims to bind the shocking experience, preserving it so that it may be revisited later. This is simply a way of restating Freud's theory of trauma (*Nachträglichkeit*), in which the unconscious responds to a shock by deferring its impact until the child has the capacity to experience it, both mentally and emotionally.

The ordinary stuff of childhood is wide open for unconscious readings that may transform the everyday into the shocking. Being made to sing in front of the class, being forced to wrestle with another child, having one's lunchbox stolen … the child may be unable to speak these things to the parents, but the self-experience will be indelible.

Alex, in the first session of breakdown, began by recollecting a time when he was at the cinema as a twelve year old. He had kissed his girlfriend who was seated next to him. A classmate sitting behind him had said: 'Alex doesn't know how to kiss!' As soon as this was said he felt a strange kind of rumbling shock coursing through him from toes to head. His legs went wobbly, he nearly wet himself, he could barely hold himself up in the seat, and when the film was over all he could think about was how he was going to walk out of the cinema without collapsing. Deconstructing why that was such a shock took some time in the analysis, but eventually he remembered that when the event happened he had a thought that this had changed his life, he did not know what to do, and he would never be the same again

In my book *The Freudian Moment*, I maintained that the discovery of psychoanalysis, in particular the Freudian Pair (the analysand free associating; the analyst free listening),[3] was the realization of a phylogenetic preconception.[4] For thousands of years men and women had been searching unconsciously for exactly this kind of relationship, in which they could speak the dream to an 'other', who would listen and then elicit the self's own unconscious knowledge of its meaning, through the process of free association. The term 'psychoanalysis' is the conceptualization of this realization and, as a signifier, it points to a project that takes place within a certain special kind of relationship.

I believe that the child that is stunned by a disturbing event in reality has an unconscious sense, or preconception, that someday they will be able to turn to an empathic other in order to make sense of the experience. (This expectation may be founded on existing figures who are important in their life, such as good grandparents; ancient, fairy-tale people who seem endlessly loving and wise.) There is not only an unconscious belief in the arrival of this other, but also there will be a search to find such a person, within whose presence those frozen self-states can be released, then conceptualized and, finally, understood.

This preconception often appears to be realized when the self falls in love. Owing to the promise of love and the intoxicating feeling of this relationship, it is not unusual for the self to realize stored self-states in the form of powerful disclosures to the lover. The problem is that, although the lover may feel gratified and privileged initially to be gifted such precious secrets, it may not be long before they feel disturbed by it and are unsure what to do. It is not enough for their partner to have 'got it off their chest' as there has been no abreaction of the affect buried in the event. It needs to be experienced in the presence of an other, who will transform it into meaning. This is ordinarily far too much for a lover to do—although many try—and the stress of the situation can prove too much for the couple, who may even break up under the strain.

In the world of therapy, many adults will seek people who have designated themselves as ready to receive, contain and process these stored self-states. By this time, however, although some people will remember the event that originally disturbed them, many do not. It may be present as a feeling of something they know is inside them, but it cannot be thought.

All of us are composed of the unthought known. We know the world of our infancy and early childhood through unconscious experiencing. Before we have language, we lack the mental equipment to think the experiences we are having so they are stored in non-verbal representational categories— the play of light, the sound of a voice—that are composed of psychosomatic unities. In time, these may connect to one another and form the basis of emotional experience and unconscious fantasy.

Usually, once language has been acquired these preverbal self-states are transferred into the symbolic order. This means that an upsetting early experience will attach itself to words that will then bear their significance for the rest of the self's life. One patient, for example, said that whenever they heard the word 'banana' a kind of sick feeling overtook them. They did not look at bananas in shops because they did not like the sound of the word. It took a long time for this word to break down into its meanings. 'Ba' meant 'Bah!' 'Nana' meant 'Na, Na, Na!' So 'banana' carried a powerful, contemptuous 'Bah ! NO!' from the other. It was, literally, a stomach-churning event for this patient and whenever they heard the word their face would screw up with revulsion. This is a pre-verbal, bodily expression of a self-state; an infantile experience was transferred into the word 'banana' because the word captured aspects of that experience, and it was thereafter held in the symbolic order for storage and understanding.

So, before a breakdown people may seek psychotherapy because they have a feeling, from within the unthought known, that something disturbing is on its way to some form of representation. The emotional experience that constitutes the release of the unthought known in the therapeutic environment is the fulfilment of an unconscious promise that the child makes to the self. When there is finally somebody there to receive the inexplicably painful, the confusing, the horrifying, most people, who are occupied by deeply disturbing self-states, will break down.

This brings us to the oft-repeated anti-psychoanalytic remark that psychoanalysis makes people worse, or that it is the disease that promotes itself as the cure. There is no question that, in many cases, when people arrive for psychoanalysis this event will trigger the movement of inner trauma toward mental realization and eventual understanding. And there is no question that the structure of the psychoanalytical process is set up to elicit this emergence so that it may contain and transform it. However, it is incorrect to suggest that psychoanalysis is the cause of the crisis. Such breakdowns will happen eventually, either inside the evocative action of a relationship or when there is a new shock to the self in external life.

One of the most important tasks facing the analyst is to discover in minute detail the event that precipitated the person's breakdown. Once that event has been deconstructed and analysed meticulously then the analysand can shift from a position of mental chaos, pain and deep anxiety into the realm of historical understanding.

Even when it becomes clear how the self's unconscious interpreted the event, this does not automatically resolve the anxieties that are present. What it does achieve, however, is the start of a binding process—the containment and organization of anxieties—which is the formal effect of interpretive understanding. The act of interpretation offers new ideas to be thought but, in addition to the *content* it delivers, it is also a way of giving *form* to what has been disclosed from the patient's unconscious. As it gives structure to chaos, this formal effect is profoundly important to the ego, which is concerned first and foremost not with meaning but with organization.

That said, unless the interpretations are sufficiently correct the binding process will not be successful. If the analysand is misunderstood, this will threaten to create a false organization that will increase anxiety and distrust of the analyst's holding capability. This is why I have stressed the need to be meticulous in gathering the details of the event, before one can gradually discover the patterns of meaning that are revealed through the process of free association and further analytical questioning.

In my experience, the precipitating event invariably encapsulates the unconscious frailty of the patient. Once understood, it serves as a mental portal. If the patient has been in analysis for some time, hopefully there will be many threads connecting through that portal that are already familiar to analyst and patient. Through the doors of internal perception these threads will link together the patient's past, their present circumstances and the mental structure of the self.

Chapter 8

Time

More than anything, the patient who is breaking down needs *time*.

The breakdown must be allowed time to happen, within a human relationship in which the other is there to hear from the self, and not run away from it. This experience is deeply reassuring to the parts of the patient that are panicking. But in order to accomplish this it must be clear to them that the psychoanalyst is prepared to stick it out for as long as it takes. Giving up is not an option.

In a conventional analytical session, lasting forty-five or fifty minutes, there is a spatio-temporal boundary that constitutes the analytical frame. This frame acquires a meaning in itself; it has structure, a *form* like that of a poem, a musical composition or a ritual. Whatever is said or enacted will be revealed within the form of the frame, and will thus have been shaped by it.

The analysand may be silent for a few minutes, or chat a bit before the session shifts from social reality to psychoanalytical reality. The analysand is now speaking as a form of listening to the self, as unconscious thinking arrives through the praxis of free association. The analyst immerses themself in the process of deep listening and, from time to time, 'catches the drift of the patient's unconscious with their own unconscious', discovering links in the chain of ideas, feeling the logic of the emotional experience or discerning the

movement of character in the transference.[1] This may give rise
to an interpretation or a series of observations that, in turn,
invite the analysand to reply. They may work for a while on
this: there are silences, the hour ends, and both wait until the
next session when the same process will occur in a different
form, with different contents, but within the same frame.

To take the most extreme form of treatment that I am
presenting here—the all-day session—it is clear that,
although the medium is still psychoanalysis, the temporal
frame is radically altered. A few hours into the day the
familiar form will be dissolving; the rhythmic logic of the
forty-five minute hour will gradually give way to a different
beat. Time is not so close a factor inside the session; the
analysand is no longer under its auspices in the same way.
The rhythm that emerges, an unknown temporality, will now
be determined by the analysand's mental state, and by the
truth of internal needs.

The complex of issues now emerging into consciousness
could not be fully articulated within the time allotted to a
conventional session. The shift from the law of the frame to
the demands of the *après-coup* or the ego-need, signifies to the
unconscious that psychoanalysis has understood a need for
this temporary reorientation.

The analysand realizes that there is the time and space
necessary for the self's ailment to be given a full hearing.
They gradually feel a lessening of urgency, of the pressure to
get as much said as possible. Time seems to open up and
mental space expands its capacity for holding and processing
the plenitude of mental contents and emotional states that
will be forthcoming.

This allows for more extended internal interludes, periods
of intense inner experiencing when the analysand is lost in
thought and feeling, quite unaware of the presence of the
analyst. Hours can pass with the patient in this state of mind.

I infer both from what I observe and from my own
intuition that, paradoxically, in the midst of such suffering,
these are deeply peaceful times, and patients have told me

later that such interludes were the most important part of the entire experience. They say it was akin to wakeful dreaming, with occasional hallucination-like visions, or eidetic memories, interspersed with passing lucid views of themselves, their mothers or fathers, or their life. They felt they were inside a moving process. It never occurred to them to speak whilst inside it, nor did they expect me to say anything.

When I first offered this extended analysis I had no way of knowing how long the intervention might have to last. In fact, probably the single greatest surprise to me has been how short-lived these crises were. I have found that, as long as one succeeds in catching the analysand before they fall, the severe phase of the breakdown turns out to be remarkably brief. I have never had to continue with all-day sessions for more than three days.

Over time, I came to know that even the most violent breakdown will run its course, and I learnt that breakdowns generally occur in clear stages, with a beginning, a middle period and an end. The sequence of mental events that unfolds seems to have something to do with ego timing. There is a sense within the ego that an activity has been instigated, one that has parameters and rules, an aim and a method with which to accomplish it. Just as the ego is the self's unconscious pattern-maker, it is also the agency that perceives patterns in life.

One curative dimension with people in breakdown is the maintaining of the person's connection to their life and future.

The infant ego gives way to the child's ego, and then the adolescent ego, then on from young adulthood to all the further stages of a life. It is an organization that, over time, develops its own sense of the tasks it faces in the present, structuring the psychic complexes it inherits from the past, and envisioning the stages to come. This ability to sense the future may be phylogenetic, part of the collective unconscious, or the brain's wired knowledge.

We all have a mental investment in the future. We need it because life is difficult. The human experience—our passage through the lifespan—is full of the unexpected, the unanticipated, for better or for worse. The future is not only an imaginary moment, it is an ego-aim: to get the self through the present into whatever is to come. Each second of our existence accomplishes this: no sooner is the future achieved than it is transformed into the past. The individual feels that they are on the move in life, and that this is good. The ego senses the self's life-span as a temporal structure.

If I had said to these patients at the outset, 'Forget about the future. Forget about your life. We shall stay with this even if it takes years', the patients would have had real reason to interpret this, not as confidence but as omnipotence, and this would have increased their anxiety. Most importantly, a crucial curative object relation would have been discarded. My patients and I always had in mind that there was a world waiting for them to which they would return. They had a sense that the future would be a good place to be in the weeks to come, once they had worked through elements from the past that had held them back.

As the ego accepts the breakdown of its defences in the analysis, its signal anxieties and primary anxieties are allayed by the psychoanalytical process. The ego unfreezes the sources of mental pain so that the self is now flushed with emotional truths. As the analyst indicates their appreciation of the ego's capacities, the person can see that they have attributes and ways of dealing with life that are sources of strength. This allows self and ego to operate under that kind of negative capability that we might term *ego faith*.

Contrast this with the situation of the schizophrenic. One of the tragedies of chronic schizophrenia is that only primitive, core ego functioning is operating, and this is not reliable. The past is a dream, and the self does not want to remember it or speak it because this turns the dream into a nightmare. Since the future exists only as a black hole, the self tries to live in a perpetual waking present: gazing at the

TV, sitting in a chair, walking down a hall, defecating, urinating, eating ... these moments are not distinguished in time but are part of endlessness. In all these different situations the self will behave with the same mentality; its aim is just to be and to be undisturbed. The night is fearful, but medications await and may dope the self so there are no dreams, no waking in the night to an absent world.

Set against the tragedy of schizophrenia, the person who has a breakdown is fortunate. As the psychoanalyst conveys that the present terrifying experience is temporary and will not last more than a few weeks, the self's ego can start to envision and map out its future. And, of course, that map will change as ego assumptions shift with the transformations accomplished in analysis.

Chapter 9

Emotional experience

When a person is breaking down the process can go one of two ways.

In the majority of cases, there is time for patient and analyst to start to make historical links, and to explore the significance of the precipitating event before the full force of the breakdown takes hold and creates a situation of deep regression. The analysand devolves slowly into breakdown with the increased analytic provision.

On occasions, however, the sudden arrival of overwhelmingly powerful emotion pre-empts the analytic pair's exploration of recent and past history. When this happens it is likely, in my view, to indicate a breaking through of experiences that originated before language. This means that the unthought known that is being released in the here and now cannot be historicized, at least not at first.

Here, one has to respect the ego's intelligence of presentation. If the patient begins with language, reflection, recollection of recent events and links them to the past, this will pave the way for the stored emotional experiences to find their route to expression. If, however, the patient begins with the depths of emotional experience, then the analyst must accept this fact and not try to divert the situation; for example, by insisting on a discussion of the precipitating event.

We shall now explore further the nature of emotional experience during breakdown, but first it is useful to draw a few distinctions.

An emotion is not an affect.

An affect is a single internal event, usually a mental-bodily state, such as anxiety, elation, anger or fright.

There is, in fact, no such thing as *an* emotion; there are only 'emotional experiences', which will be condensations of many internal elements. An emotional experience is an organization, very much like a dream.

Attachment theorists have written a great deal about affects and how they figure in adult life. It is a useful focus, but it is important to bear in mind its limitations. Affect theory describes an infant's self-states: satisfaction, distress, anxiety, panic, rage, and so forth. As an infant grows, they begin to develop more complex emotional experiences. For example, they learn that their mother is not simply a provider of nurturance and bodily care, she is also a person with moods and habits. They will know that their own being, too, is a fluctuating variable.

There are some fairly predictable emotional experiences. For example, as the infant approaches a mealtime they see Mum preparing the food, and this sets off a series of affects, memories, wishes and expectations. Single unforeseen happenings in what is otherwise routine—a phone call, a tummy ache, Mum dropping a saucepan and swearing—will inevitably bring aleatory contributions to the sequence of events. It is all part of an increasingly sophisticated relationship to the other. An emotional experience, in infancy and at all further stages in life, is above all else *a moving experience.* It may be simple or complex, pleasant or unpleasant, and often it will be a mixture. Unlike affects, emotional experiences cannot be observed. This is possibly why the concept tends to take a back seat to affect theory in contemporary psychoanalysis. In recent years, analysts have leant increasingly towards what is evident and observable, and this is unfortunate given that the human mind is neither, but is filled with what Hannah Arendt termed 'the invisibles'.

When a patient in breakdown has an emotional experience they are inside an internal event. It may be accompanied by outward signs, such as laughter, tears, anger, fidgeting on the couch or idiosyncratic speech patterns, but it will only ever manifest itself in part, either in their own consciousness or to the other. With emotions, unlike with affects, what you see is not what you are getting.

Indeed, for both patient and analyst, an emotional experience is even more challenging to comprehend than a dream. Whereas the dream is a completed event recollected from the past, the constituents of the emotional experience are constantly moving. They involve all categories of unconscious life: body states, body senses, body memories, affects, recollected memories, desires, instinctual derivatives, ideas, fantasies, interventions by the real, the shadow of relational moments, released axioms of self-organization, the unthought knowns of our being, the arrival of introjects, and so forth.

Whether they arrive suddenly and unheralded, or after analyst and patient have begun to connect present and past events, at some point the emotional experiences frozen in psychic time are freed, and they rush into the present. The sheer force of this impact is the most astonishing thing I have witnessed in my clinical work. However relaxed I may be feeling, the moment when the deferred affect explodes into the room is always overwhelming. It is what was and now is. It needs no commentary. The mental pain of the individual's suffering is now being released through memory, understanding and evoked emotional experience, and the analyst has just to be there, listening and learning.

These phenomena are usually at their most intense within the all-day sessions, when they are unconstrained by the limits of time. It feels impossible to convey this intensity in words, and I am aware that I have not done it justice in my clinical examples. The emotional experience is enormously complex, involves the full range of inner experience and cannot be simplified into a single organized idea. It is more like a dream without manifest content; a poem without words; the wind moving through a landscape and animating the natural world. It allows the analysand's emotional life to become the force of cure.

When they come from this core of deep experiencing, the analysand's free associations or lucid statements will alter. The talking self will have been saturated in prolonged waves of emotion that will never be worded in themselves, but all that is then said to the analyst will be saturated with significance.

Looking back on this aspect of these longer sessions, some analysands have said that the physicality of the room became essential to them, as though they were bathed in light and sound. Could this be recalling life within the womb, when light and sound were experienced as phenomena-in-themselves? Might these long private interludes in some way provide a re-birthing of the self; an experiential shift in which the self moves back into unthought-known memories of foetal life and early infantile experience?

As well as memories of their history and many other forms of representational musing, I do believe that, in breakdown, analysands experience the basic elements of being human, the thing-in-itself of their existence. Hence their absorption in the essentials of existence: sound, light, colour, scent and images.

These are not moments for rolling insights, the hubbub of dialogue, the articulation of the formations of the self's character through the transference or countertransference. Indeed, it is as if these ordinary features of analysis become mere asides, as self opens up to the most fundamental dimension of *being*.

Of course, there is pain here; elemental pain about existence and the suffering endemic to being human. People cry, scream, yell, thrash about. They employ all the forms open to them to be who they are. We may think of these states, not as projective identifications but as *projective objectifications*. In the hellish moments of a breakdown there are times when the analysand seems to be objectifying themself, asking some god why they are the thing that they are. Yet nothing is projected that is not held in common between all people. What is projected is the elemental: the 'thingness' of being a living being.

The long silences following such intensities may perhaps be recognitions of this primal thingness. One patient said she felt that all aspects of being herself were pushing up, through her, into her mind; at times it was as if she were in a theatre, watching herself as a mutative being, forming and transforming before her senses.

These experiential interludes may be followed by a return to anguish, to the attack on the self, brought about by breakdown. To describe it as attack seems more accurate than to suggest that the people are simply in conflict with themselves. When patients speak to the analyst there is often an implicit plea for help in removing something that is overwhelming them, something they have carried all their lives. Now at last it is outside the self, they can see it more clearly, and when they shudder from the suffering it has imposed upon them, they want help in getting rid of it. They objectify projectively what it means to be in ordinary human forms of hell.

These long sessions seem to allow for a paradoxical temporal distortion. Hours of silence are experienced as brief, whereas the intervening bouts of intense anguish and emotional catharsis, lasting in reality for only fifteen or twenty minutes, are experienced by the patient as going on for hours.

Chapter 10

Reflection, explanation and working through

Reflective states have a particular quality in these extended sessions. Of course there is more time in which thoughts can evolve, but it is more than that. The reflections that occur during a breakdown, following long periods of deep internal work and bouts of intense pain, are not simply reflective but *integrative*.

To be sure, all reflection may contribute to integration. Examining the self, we look into an internal mirror and discover things we had not seen before, which enlarge our self-understanding and become part of our unconscious structure. However, it seems that the reflectiveness that happens during these extended sessions expands perceptual potentials in a particular way: it allows for wider visions into one's self and deeper penetrations into the self's history, inner world and objectified structures. So much that has previously been unconscious is now coming up into consciousness, so that the individual needs a slowed-down form of perception to allow for slower and deeper reflective work.

Think of the dream. It is the accomplishment of the dreamwork, most notably, from the process of condensation. In the course of ordinary psychoanalysis, unravelling the meaning of a powerful and compelling dream may take hours of free association, over a period of days. A breakdown is not so dissimilar to a dream, in that consciousness and the self's executive abilities are overwhelmed by the emergence of a crippling complex of memories, ideas, emotions and axioms that are deeply enigmatic.

The dream and breakdown are both highly encrypted moments, events that it will take time to decode. It is not a matter of intellection but of immersion in the material, in order that the mind can elaborate the encoded condensations through further unconscious work, laced with emotional experience and insights. Compared with the dream, however, the enigma of breakdown causes much greater suffering. Like the riddle of the Sphinx, it requires high-level properties of the mind to decipher it. The work of understanding is, therefore, simultaneous and coexistent with the recovery of the self's mind. To understand the enigma is to recover one's sanity.

For decades, Freud believed that if unconscious conflicts were made conscious, this would cure neurosis. This Post-Enlightenment idea was later abandoned by him when he discovered that, even though the many resistances might be overcome, this process was not necessarily transformative in itself.

It seemed that enlightenment was not enough.

Freud's attention then turned to transference, and to the notion that even though patient and analyst might throw light on a symptom or a character issue, it had to be enacted in the relationship with the analyst for it to be fully analysed. The analyst had to become part of the problem before they could begin to be part of the cure. The event of the transference was then to be translated into consciousness, and the combination of the experienced and the thought had transformative potential.

However, it would appear that Freud's first idea, that heightened consciousness of the source of a person's problem would transform it, can be true, but only in very special circumstances.

Thus far, in considering the sequence of events in working with a person who is breaking down, we have discussed the role of the analytical frame and method, the establishment of a contract between patient and analyst, and the particular, intense quality of the interaction: the intermittent, brief dialogues, long periods of silence, and the patient's emotional experiencing.

Now we come to the issue of explanation.

It is the analyst's obligation to put, in lucid and memorable terms, the exact reasons why a person is having a breakdown, and why they are the way they are, in relation to their psychic history. This will include a clear description of the defences they have employed up until now.

Whilst it is true to say that this is a form of interpretation, it is more accurately an *explanation*, a full and complete one that allows the analysand to grasp consciously, and in plain English, why all this is happening. As people are, generally, very distraught at this time, and it can be very hard for them to take things in, I have, on occasion, written down for them a one- or two-page description of the total situation.

No doubt many of my colleagues will disagree with this deviation from standard technique. How could I resort to putting in writing a psychoanalytic explanation of the relation between life history and mental state? Surely such an understanding should evolve out of a process of co-constructive working through?

What is my premise?

During a breakdown, patients will give an account of its onset that will link to their past and evoke powerful emotional experiences. But in order for this to be transformative they need to know consciously how all the elements fit together into a gestalt; they need to comprehend how they are a composition of their lives. Provided it is clear, simply expressed and to the point, the written explanation constitutes a *lucid object* that will be read and digested again and again by the analysand. They will bring to it many thematic variations, but it will have a coherence that they value highly, as it carries within it the core truths of their life.

Through this repetition the patient might seem to be learning something by rote rather than by reflection, but in fact the frequent revisiting of the explanation immerses the self in the matrix of its psychic truth. The past, transformed into the structure of their history, has been linked to the event that crystallized that past and stimulated the breakdown. This has allowed the deferred affect, connected to the original events, to be released and this, in turn, emotionally informs the fears and distresses of the present. The self is now being instructed from within, and what has felt frightening or shattering is now filled with a much thicker emotional knowledge.

Heightened consciousness functions as a transitional act, collecting the many sources of released unconscious news— existential experiences from the recent and distant past, emotional movement, free associations—into a lucid object of thought that ties together the threads from the unconscious. The binding activity of narrative form allows the analysand to have a different type of conversation with the self; they can talk to themselves about how this all makes sense.

The lucid explanation, then, objectifies the self's core disturbance and becomes a transitional mental object, aiding the self's development of a new psychic structure. During the breakdown, this structure—a new way of perceiving the self and the world—will be held in consciousness. Then, as the patient recovers, conscious memory and understanding of the reasons for breakdown will fade. If the analyst has written down the explanation, it will be lost or discarded. What was learned will seem to have vanished, but over time the analyst will note changes in the analysand's axioms of thinking, being and relating. The explanations, previously brought into consciousness but now forgotten, have become part of the self's mental structure as operational assumptions. There has been a transformative communication between the unconscious and the conscious self.

I shall give a few examples of what I mean by lucid statements.

Clara had a depressive breakdown after being sacked from her job. Her boss, Oswald, was a sadistic man and no one had lasted more than a year in her post, but she was devastated. Her entire family were achievers and all her brothers and sisters were highly successful. In her early thirties, she had never been in a relationship because she 'had no time'. At the beginning of our work she was distant, short-tempered, sceptical about psychoanalysis and highly critical of me.

After we had pieced together elements of her childhood, history and recent events, she dissolved from a removed and arrogant position into intense sadness, grief and prolonged crying. I made the following statement:

> You are depressed not only because Oswald fired you but also because the harsh, driven part of you agreed with him. For your entire life you have identified with the achieving part of the family and, as neither mother nor father had room for feelings or intimacy—that was for 'losers'—you have denigrated your own needs and vulnerabilities. When I brought them up in our work, I became the target of the Oswald part of you and I experienced what it was like to be on the receiving end of loathing. You have always been running to keep ahead of that depression that was bound to catch up with you, because your external achievements can never be enough to provide for your emotional needs.

Clara took in every word of this. Over the ensuing days I repeated it in many different ways and she talked about it in great detail:

'How did you know my family were only into achievement?'

'You told me.'

'I did?'

'Yes.'

'It's funny, but I guess I can't remember it.'

'Because you don't listen to yourself.'

'I don't listen to myself?'

'You have contempt, like your parents, for those who say things. Only "doing" brings accolades. So you admire what you accomplish but you don't listen to what you say.'

Brief conversations such as this would elucidate the explanation. It was part of the 'working through' that now became part of the analysand's intellection. Clara's questions were verbalizations of potential axioms that would be internalized during this process of working through. They would then become part of a transformed mental structure that would change the way she governed her life. Before such restructuralization could take place, however, she needed to 'use the object', to work over the themes embedded in the explanation, to question every aspect of it. It was discussed and rediscussed many times, between the long periods of silence that occupied five intense weeks of extended analysis, before she was free.

Another example.

Helen grew up in a family of pleasant people who worked hard and were kind, but who shut away any intimate connections they might have had with one another. She was sent off to boarding school from the ages of eight to fourteen, and was rarely visited by either parent. She spent summers at home with local friends, watched a lot of TV, and life seemed to be good enough. After university she married Toby, they had three children, and Helen worked as a copy editor at her local newspaper.

She presented as a very bubbly, upbeat person. She had many friends, mainly through her involvement with a busy local church, and she fancied she was 'good with people' because they often sought her advice. She liked to see herself as 'an unlicensed life coach', but she avoided self-reflection, and had neither insight into herself nor interest in her past. She came for analysis in her mid-fifties because she had been having panic attacks that seemed to come out of nowhere. When they occurred she would then dive into a depression for days on end, wondering what was the matter with her.

In the first year of the analysis it was striking that she produced no memories at all of her first ten years of life. Descriptions of her parents were colourless, so when she let it slip that her mother had disappeared for about fifteen months when she was eight, it was really quite shocking.

'She disappeared?'

'Yeah, I guess so.'

'You don't know?'

'No, I do. She disappeared.'

After a silence of a few minutes, Helen proceeded to tell me about a social event planned for that evening, a church outing for the following week, and various other matters. We had ten minutes left in the session.

'Your mother has disappeared again.'

'I beg your pardon?'

'She left your description without notice and went missing as you moved on to talk about other things.'

'Well … I mean. I told you. I thought, well, that's it.'

'You thought, "that's it?"'

'Yeah, I guess so.'

'Easy come, easy go …'

'Well, I don't know. I can't remember it.'

'I appreciate that, but right here and now you were remembering a rather amazing fact—your mother disappeared for fifteen months—and then she dropped out of the session.'

'Was I supposed to do it differently?'

'You feel I am being critical of you.'

'No, not really. But I am aware that you seem rather shocked.'

'Indeed, that is true. But you don't permit yourself to be shocked.'

This vignette is typical of the sessions we had before her breakdown. Even though she claimed to have no recollections, she would suddenly come up with a stunning memory.

Three years into analysis Toby left her. He had been having an affair for ten years and, as Helen discovered, everyone had known about this except her.

She was deeply shocked; she had no idea he was unhappy and had 'never seen this coming'. Her husband repeated again and again why things had not worked for him in the marriage, saying he felt she was so out of touch with him that he could no longer bear it. However, she refused to accept her husband's departure and, certain that she could win him back, she began to rehearse scenes of reconciliation. They would meet at the market or bump into one another at church, she would fall into his arms, they would be back together.

Helen was in an agitated depression. I had set up a care system and she was seeing me twice a day for ninety-minute sessions, seven days a week. Since she was unable to sleep, the psychiatrist prescribed sleeping medication and, as her panic attacks during the day were very severe, we also agreed that she should have Valium on hand, in case she was unable to calm herself.

Soon, memories began to flood into the analysis and she was overwhelmed. She would go in and out of states of primary anxiety and I would help her recover by saying that it was completely understandable that she should be so distraught, that she had wonderful assets and was courageous, and that we would make it through this.

At a crucial stage in her breakdown it was possible to provide her with a lucid explanation. I said:

> You have avoided many things in your life. You have focused on your work, the children, and your friends at church, but you steer clear of anything troubling. This has meant keeping a distance, not only from other people but from yourself too. You are afraid to look into yourself because, with all the stuff going on in your family, and all the feelings inside you about being put into exile, you could only survive as a kid by not looking at what was there in you. Now, when you are in an acutely painful situation, you are trying to use your mind to displace reality.

Helen needed many repetitions of this explanation. At first, she responded by acting out, confronting her husband at his workplace, dolled-up in a sexy outfit, and imploring him to come back to her. In the following session she said:

'I mean you would agree, wouldn't you, that it is possible we can get back together?'

'That your mind can make things so?'

'No, I mean I could get him back if I ... I just know there are certain ways to do this. You would agree with that in principle, wouldn't you?'

'I agree that a child abandoned to school has to believe there must be a way to get out of this when reality does not change.'

'But I mean, just asking you a theoretical question, not about my husband, are you saying there's no way to get people back?'

'No, I'm not saying that.'

'So, you agree that it's possible.'

'In the abstract, yes. In reality, in your reality, I am sorry to say, but no I don't agree. That is my feeling, but I don't have a crystal ball.'

'Okay, but that does mean it is still possible that my husband will change his mind, so you are agreeing with me now?'

'I think you are so eager for your mind to force reality to be the way you want it, that you are trying to coerce me into compliance with your wishes.'

'I don't think I am doing that. I think I'm just trying to get something clear here because I value what you say highly.'

'I think you're in great pain, and you're showing me how you believe your mind can make up a reality.'

'But that is just your opinion, correct?'

'Yes, it is just my view.'

'You might be wrong about this.'

'Yes, my mind does not determine reality any more than yours.'

For some days, our conversations proceeded like this, sometimes throughout an entire ninety minutes, and Helen's agitation was extreme. But after six weeks of work, the consistency of the explanation started to function as a transitional psychic phenomenon. When she acted out she would say, 'I know what you are going to say …', and I would reply, 'You mean, you know what *you* are going to say', and so it would go on. At that point the explanation was simply an introject – they were my words but gradually they became *concepts* that Helen understood as accurate translations of her present and her past. Eventually, they became her property, and as this occurred she emerged from her breakdown.

At the end of her analysis, Helen recalled the breakdown as a powerful and life-changing event. By then her understanding of the precise issues had waned and become vague comments about being overattached and too anxious. What were in place, however, were new mental structures. She looked regularly into her inner world, reported dreams and thought about what was going on. She had fewer friends than before, as the hypomanic quality to her relationships had declined, but her friendships grew deeper as she became more rooted.

The sorts of conversations described above may not seem much like conventional analysis. Yet, in such situations, analyst and patient *are* working something through, and doing so quite consciously.

The work of the philosopher/psychologist Radu Bogdan may help us understand how psychoanalysis functions at this level.[1] He presents an interesting theory about the 'mentamental' (about the mental) and of 'reflexivity' (a mind thinking about its own thoughts), predicated on the development, from childhood to adulthood, of relationships between minds. He would argue, I think, that by engaging the patient in this way one is developing the analysand's *inter*mental capability, which will lead eventually to increased *intra*mental ability.

I find this a helpful way to help conceptualize these issues, and most analysts would probably agree with it, at least in part. However, Bogdan ignores completely the demand made upon a mind by the dream. By focusing on the dream as the *Ur* mental event that sponsors associations and predictions, Freud's theory of reflexivity goes much deeper than the simple internalization of mental engagements with others. While certain aspects of the work I have presented here can be described in Bogdanian terms, the crux of this form of analytical working through is the consistent linking of the analysand's conscious thought process to their unconscious life. By engaging with the analyst's mind—developing intermental capacities that become intramental structures—the patient is also promoting the relationship between consciousness and unconsciousness, between two different ways of thinking that influence one another. This activity lends to consciousness an object relational impetus that has been missing or underused in the lives of these analysands.

The exchanges between analyst and analysand in such moments may seem to be simply dialogical, to exemplify external behaviour. In fact, I think they are a way of illuminating *mental experience*. While it is, of course, impossible to read another person's mind, this kind of dialogue comes close to a theatrical soliloquy. As James Hirsh points out, the soliloquy was never intended to illustrate how we talk internally; we do not talk to ourselves in this way.[2] But it does exemplify something about mental life.

The intermental activities exemplified above allow analysands to observe and experience *in situ* the way in which they think. They do not so much hear their thoughts as experience their mental process. By doing this, repeatedly, their mentality becomes sufficiently enacted to become an object of perspectival consideration. In turn, although the analyst may introduce specific ideas, or content, more importantly they are demonstrating the *form* in which the psychoanalytical mind functions, indicating a particular way of thinking about the self. This gradually enables the patient to understand how their mind works, which patterns of thought typify them, and how these have misdirected them at crucial moments.

Much is made of consciousness theory these days, and too often the illusion is promoted unwittingly that consciousness is self-determining. In fact, even if we are focused on a task that seems bound by the logic of its agenda, the connecting links between moments of consciousness are always unconscious. There is, at best, a disconnected parallel between the flow of conscious ideas and the underlying unconscious thinking. Detailed study of the free associative process shows clearly that the stream of conscious thoughts is unconsciously determined.

Even scientists, the nominated guardians of objectivity, will admit that, although they may follow a rigorous path of consciously determined observation, the moment of breakthrough—the sudden arrival of lucid thinking—often strikes them from out of the blue. For all the labours of consciousness, it is unconscious thinking that is the source and the guide of personal creativity, and in all psychoanalyses there is a fascinating intimacy between consciousness and unconscious thought.

I have stressed the value of providing a lucid summary that explains to the person why they are in a state of breakdown, and often leads to a series of challenging discussions in the realm of what Bogdan terms 'intermental relations'. As thoughts are exchanged, minds are expanded and exercised, and the patient is now actively using conscious thought where before they may have reflected very little upon their life.

Even if the patient's thoughts seem defence-driven, wish-laden or endlessly repetitive, if the analyst engages them in this intermental activity then the groundwork is set for transformative substantive explanations that will be structuralized by the patient. Importantly, however, the patient will have found a way to think their thoughts to themself, predicated on a dialectical procedure that allows for mind to experience all of its realities in a highly dynamic way. Their mind will then engage both with other minds and with the object world. It will also be ready to receive unconscious mental contents and unconscious ways of thinking, so that a new intramental activity is set up; not between two competing conscious sets of thinking, but between conscious and unconscious.

Chapter 11

Psychic change

The rationale behind the method I am proposing is predicated on the assumption that, if a psychoanalyst or a psychotherapist can sense when patients are in the early stages of a mental breakdown, then they can catch them before they decompensate.

I am suggesting that the breakdown is a psychological necessity mandated by the arrival of deferred issues, from events experienced during the self's early life, or from a disintegration owing to weaknesses in the ego. Although this abruption may be a terrifying event, both for the patients themselves and for their friends and family, the encounter with deeply meaningful memories, mental strategies and painful emotions from the past can transform the impending catastrophe into a potential space for profound change.

Looking back to Emily, Anna, and Mark certain things are clear insofar as psychic change is concerned.

With the arrival of previously concealed, powerful emotional facts comes a near-direct communication from the self's child-held traumas and longstanding inner vulnerabilities. Of necessity, this means that a person in a breakdown will regress, and often alarmingly so. Anna lost bowel function. Mark's sobbing was the howling of a hybrid man-infant. The sheer force of the self-in-breakdown can be harrowing unless the analyst has made adequate provision for containing the situation.

The intensification of suffering afforded the analysis an unusual opportunity to be effective because of the patient's strikingly increased need for analytic care. At the outset this involved an adaptation on the analyst's part: increased number of sessions; extended sessions; a team of people helping out. This provided a holding environment that was able both to meet the analysand's present needs, and to provide a different object from the one that had been part of the patient's early psychic history.

Emily's mother and father abandoned her to relatives when she was a small child. Anna's mother could not find in her the sort of daughter she desired, and they developed a cold relationship that was mitigated by the father's idealization; something that she had continued to bank on for the rest of her life. Mark's mother was weak and his father remote and sometimes cruel, but he knew that he used his parents' failures as lancets with which to punish them. He responded by developing an isolated self, strategically aimed at counter-cruelty: he would lock the other out of his life.

As these patients crumbled, as a result in part of rejections by people that they loved, their defensive strategies failed and they were returned to the original traumas that had created a basic fault in their personalities. I am convinced that years of analysis of those defences were spared because the intensity of the crisis was met there and then by analytic understanding of their needs.

Emily crashed into a ball of fury that I endured and linked to its origin. Even though her sense of self remained somewhat wobbly, she emerged a less cold, rigid individual, more emotionally connected with other people. When Anna accepted the care provided she fell to pieces, but her acute intellectual grasp allowed her to use my interpretations as transformative objects. Mark's desolation was unprecedented in his adult life but, although his world was caving in around him, he could appreciate that this was a hugely important event in his life. Transforming the raw scars of the past into an emotionally coherent history was deeply relieving and integrating. Disparate parts of his personality came together, and a man whose self-understanding had been very limited suddenly found himself making sense.

In each case, these transformative moments changed axioms that had been fundamental to that person's view of the world and their positioning of the self. Emily abandoned the assumption that in order to survive one had to form an attachment to an equally distressed other. Her mental structure now allowed her to be free of such attachments and, however vulnerable this freedom made her feel, it opened the self to richer experiences in life.

Anna abandoned the axiom that worth was to be found in the self only through the other's adoration of her accomplishments. In its place was a new realization that she never was an ideal being and that the recognition of her imperfections was a merciful relief. This brought empathy for herself but also for others.

Mark had lived according to the axiom that 'an eye-for-an-eye' must be the immediate response to any hint of rejection; he must close the door on the self's capacity to love. This left him with an illusion of power and direction but, in reality, it resulted in a closeted and narrowed emotional universe. When he found that he could allow love to remain following rejection, this enabled him to connect with the mental pain—long ago split off—of loving the mother and the father.

It is not possible to say how long the patient will take to get to this point. Perhaps unsurprisingly, those patients who received all-day sessions did change more quickly and, in some ways, more deeply than people with whom I worked with extended analysis over a longer period of time. Other variables appear to have something to do with the nature of the person's psychopathology, although this does not always seem to be the case.

If anything dictates the recovery rate, I think it may be the astuteness with which I have read the signs of breakdown and the appropriateness of my chosen strategy. But it also depends on the analysand's capacity for ego transformation: the speed with which they can move from defending the self's ailment against understanding (interpreted as a threat to the self's safety) via the transformational function of the psychoanalysis of breakdown which dissolves ego defences, to the discovery of a newly forged path for the self.

After the analysand recovers from the breakdown a rather curious thing happens ... or rather, it does not. The patient seems to have almost no memory of what took place, or of where they were during these intense periods of time. This is in part, no doubt, because the experience is not verbally explicable, but there seems to me to be another factor. It is as if a form of protective amnesia—like childhood amnesia— enfolds the patient, who then moves on in life, transformed, but as though the new self was always there.

There is no defensiveness surrounding this self-state, nor do I think it is because the person has forgotten that they have endured profound experiences. I think it is that the process which has taken place, which entered consciousness in various forms, has now returned to unconscious life and to a new ego organization. The conscious self can recall that they were broken down, but few memories remain of the emotional experiences that were part of this remarkable breakthrough.

It may have been a breakthrough, but it is also one of the most harrowing experiences anyone can have. Once they emerge from it, people are eager to move on. They re-enter everyday life, sometimes tentatively at first, but then with vigorous involvement. Instructive, transformative and terrible, the collapse is now in the past. It is not to be retained as an iconic moment.

The resumption of the previous pattern of the analysis— the customary hours, the usual amounts of time—is embraced with relief, and I have never heard a patient pine over the loss of the intensity that had occurred during their breakdown. I see this as a good sign, an indication that they have 'used the object', and that under the auspices of the life instinct they can leave it behind.

When mental breakdown is met with psychoanalysis, the self is provided with a sentient, patient, committed and understanding other. For this to appear at such a moment of acute need is profoundly curative of both present and past.

Chapter 12

Conclusion

No psychoanalysis is ordinary. In the course of a career the analyst will be struck by the remarkably different ways in which people occupy the space and use the process.

Nonetheless, there are constants. There is the frame— forty-five minutes, four or five times a week, over several years in a consistent space—and the process; the patient talking freely without searching for meaning, the analyst listening freely with no conscious agenda. The conventional psychoanalytic structure will, generally speaking, be more than adequate to handle an analysand's regressions and clinical needs, with a slow easing of ego defences and resistances, allowing archaic assumptions to be deployed in the transference.

This book has advocated, in a certain situations, an alteration in the analytic frame, *but not the process*. The new structure is set in place temporarily, in order to help the analysand through a crisis and then allow a return to the reliability of the ordinary contract.

Even the most highly experienced analyst will feel anxious when confronted by the sorts of situations described here. This signal anxiety is a vital psychic indicator, which naturally leads the clinician to consider how the patient's needs can be met under the changed clinical circumstances. Some clinicians will think immediately of referral to a colleague for medication that will target the problem and, hopefully, alleviate the analysand's distressing state. Others will arrange for a period of hospitalization. However, the reader will recognize by now that I regard mental breakdown, within the context of a psychoanalysis, as a potentially transformative event that can lead to a mental breakthrough if the analyst simply provides more psychoanalysis.

In my view, hospitalizing an analysand who is breaking down is a psychological disaster. While it may relieve the patient's toxic state of mind in the short term, it is akin to putting one's children into foster care because one is unable to manage them. Indeed, meeting up with a series of white-robed staff in an antiseptic ward is akin to being rebirthed in a non-human environment. If they want their patient to avoid the traumatic *après-coup* of a hospitalization, I believe that the analyst has no choice.

If they do take on this task themself, it is the psychoanalyst's responsibility to explain clearly why they are advocating changes in the frame. There may be some resistance at first, and I regard this as an important indicator of ego-strength; of the analysand's wish to remain within their life and to use their traditional means of coping with distress. But analysands who are in an acute crisis will usually accept these alterations almost immediately, making use of the additional time for as long as it takes for the breakdown to run its course.

I have recommended that every clinician who works this way should form a team that will assist analyst and patient through this challenging time. Even if the psychoanalyst is also a psychiatrist it is important that another colleague be brought in to provide a second view. The outpatient team mirrors the type of care that would ordinarily be given in an in-patient setting, and it has been my experience that the support of this team makes emotional and practical sense to the patient, even if there is some initial reluctance to accept the offer.

Clearly, no recently qualified clinician should undertake work of this kind without an experienced supervisor acting as a supplementary co-clinician. I do not, however, recommend that experienced practitioners seek supervision at this time.

Once the analyst accepts the task they should be guided principally by the inherent logic of the analysand's free associations and transference usages; a vocabulary far too complex to be translated adequately for a supervisory other. However well-intended, comments by colleagues about what they think is 'really' taking place are more likely to break the analyst's vital unconscious contact with the patient.

In thirty-five years of working with people on the verge of breakdown in the manner I have described, I have never had to hospitalize a patient. That some of this is down to simple luck is no doubt true, but I believe it does tell us something about the efficacy of this extension of psychoanalysis. If I felt that intensified analytical treatment was not working I would not hesitate to admit a patient to hospital. It has just never happened.

Winnicott saw the dismantling of false self-defences as a requisite for a successful analysis and he, therefore, viewed regression as meritorious in itself. There were many clinical situations in which his analysands became deeply dependent on him, giving up on high level functioning—work, family obligations, and so forth—in the interests of discovering a sense of 'personal reality', or the true self.

However, there can be serious pitfalls if one prioritizes this sense of personal reality over the ability to live in the external world. Whilst Winnicott—as well as Balint, Khan, Coltart and others—may have been expert in handling ordinary regression to dependence, I believe that promoting a state of deep, primitive dependence on the analyst is injudicious and counterproductive.

All along in my work with a patient in breakdown I discuss their ego health: their skills in their work life, successes in their relationships, the strengths of their idiom, and so forth. I do this because the crisis will cause them to lose sight of their assets, and if this situation is sustained then they can be lost to a malignant regression. The breakdown then becomes the starting point for life-long debilitation.

Referring to their assets is rather like keeping an imaginary companion in the room. That companion is the self's healthy and vital being. If one does not lose sight of this, and refers to it often, this vital being is transformed into the central object of dependence. Since the analyst is invested with the task of managing the frame and arranging the holding environment, they are projectively invested with the residual presence of a mothering and fathering figure of profound magnitude. But they must never assume these roles *at the expense* of the patient's ego health. It is crucial for all analysands—whether in ordinary treatment or in this intensified analysis—to be aware of and dependent on their own assets, rather than to relinquish the creativity of the self and depend on the care of the psychoanalyst.

Winnicott would, no doubt, disagree with my emphasis on the positive features of the patient's adaptive repertoire. So, too, would many contemporary analysts. While interpretation of resistances, defences, transferential communications and unconscious fantasies is de rigeur, there is precious little in the literature about the analyst's responsibility to give direct attention to the analysand's ego assets, whether as a character, as a relational being or as a working person.

Of course, the destructive sides of any person can envy the self's positive attributes, in which case hatred of the analyst may intensify if these are highlighted. Some patients will accuse the analyst of being insincere or trying to 'fob them off'. However, these reactions seem to be less frequent when patients are in a state of breakdown than in ordinary analysis. When an individual feels bereft and abandoned by the self, there is palpable relief when such links are made to the healthy aspects, and this becomes a valuable form of object relation between the disturbed and generative parts of the self.

The single most important relationship any of us has is to our own self. Hard as it is to conceptualize this, I think William James and Herbert Meade were close to it when discussing the relation between the 'I' and the 'me'. When a person is in breakdown it is as if the 'me' is lost, or as if there is no way to speak to it or to represent it. By describing the self's positive aspects the analyst is directly addressing the self's 'me', even as the patient has lost contact with it, or has turned away from it out of disappointment or hate.

I should make the point that the methodology explored in this book is not intended as an invitation to the patient population. The overwhelming majority of my analysands have never been aware of my providing extended sessions or intensified psychoanalysis, and this is one of the reasons I have hitherto neither discussed this nor written about it in England. I certainly do not recommend that clinicians, who are interested in pursuing this extension of analysis, offer it as an option to colleagues or patients.

This brings me to another key issue. What does one do with the analysand who requests, indeed perhaps demands, intensified analysis? From time to time the analyst will encounter a person who is gratifed by the idea of extra sessions, and indeed may act out in ways that would seem to warrant it. I have taken up some aspects of this issue in my book *Hysteria*, and I will not repeat in detail here the reasons why I would not comply with such a demand. I should emphasize, though, that the aim of the work presented in this book is to help a person from breakdown to breakthrough, not to be complicit in an enactment actualized for the dramatic deployment of the self's internal world, as a form of manipulation.

There are thus certain individuals for whom I would not recommend extended analysis: in particular, anyone presenting as a malignant hysteric, who will experience regression as a gratifying end in itself. One would also have to think carefully about extended sessions with severe paranoid and borderline patients. I think the differential here is the degree to which an impending breakdown is opening this person up to parts of their personality that have been sealed through borderline or paranoid defences.

Some of the questions that have, no doubt, been raised in reader's minds will be addressed in the next chapter, which has been reserved for frequently asked questions.

Chapter 13

Questions

With Sacha Bollas

SB: One of your premises is that these intensified sessions are simply an extension of an ordinary analysis, but this is not an ordinary analytical experience. So, can you clarify what you mean by this?

CB: There is no change to the way the analyst listens to the analysand, attends to the logic of the free associations, the moves of character, and all other aspects of an ordinary analysis. Indeed, keeping the extended session ordinary is essential to the analyst remaining the same constant object they were before this alteration of the frame.

SB: But when you bring in a psychiatrist, a social worker, a driver, this is surely a *dramatic* departure from what one would term an ordinary analysis, is it not?

CB: I understand that it might seem rather a dramatic departure from conventional practice. However, to the patient who is inside the breakdown these are experienced not as radical shifts but as essential adaptations. If the patient finds it too dramatic, one has very likely failed in one's assessment of the situation.

SB: Area Team Social Workers no longer exist in England in the way they did in the 1970s, and there are many countries where what you propose would be impossible for various reasons. Do you see any other ways in which the support team you gathered could be accomplished in today's environment?

CB: The presence of a psychiatrist to back up the analytical pair is very important. It is true that we do not have Social Services in the UK in the way that we once did—a very sad state of affairs—but the management side of things now falls within the widening sphere of psychiatrists. If they determine that others should be involved in this process—such as members of the family or friends or, for example, a nurse—then they will assume a co-ordinating function.

SB: Going back to issues of technique, many people would argue that it is not psychoanalytical for the psychoanalyst to communicate any special investment in making things better for the patient. You have written elsewhere that the goal of psychoanalysis is free association, but here it seems you are moving the goalposts; you are no longer simply analysing your patient, but responding in a way that indicates your intent to be helpful. Does that not change the analyst's role?

CB: It announces to the analysand that analysts are trained to see a patient through a breakdown, just as we are trained in how to work with people who are suicidal, severely acting out, and so on. Breakdowns may not occur in the course of most analyses, but they are nonetheless reasonably common. I think analysts all over the world will, at times, make adjustments to their usual technique, and would regard these as standard deviations.

SB: So you are talking about maintaining an analytic attitude even within changing circumstances?

CB: Yes, that is correct. Indeed I think that when the various 'schools' of analysis have presented what they think of as new techniques, many of these are, in fact, adjustments to particular clinical tasks. For example, the technical approaches to narcissistic personality disorder offered by Heinz Kohut and Otto Kernberg may seem irreconcilable, but they may both be apt for the same analysand at different moments in the course of the analysis. I think Winnicott's technique is valid for the schizoid personality, Klein's for the borderline, Lacan's for the obsessional, and so on.

SB: Could it be that your assessment of someone as being in a state of potential breakdown is a rather individual perception; that others might not see it the same way?

CB: Well, in England, and I think in Europe generally, there is little disagreement about the indications of imminent breakdown in our analysands. There is a noticeable decrease in their ability to carry out the ordinary tasks of life, accompanied by a clear increase in their sense of helplessness and severely raised levels of distress. Layers of anxiety and depression are obviously taking hold of the patient, and this soon leads a clinical depression or agitated depression, acute panic attacks, sleeping disturbances, and so on. The sight of these changes will raise signal anxiety in any analyst.

SB: But it might be objected, surely, that the clinical approach you are describing is such a highly personal feature of your work that it may be unusable by others – and unteachable.

CB: I do not believe that other well-trained analysts and therapists would be unable to work in this way. The issue I have tried to address is that too many clinicians do not know what to do when they see patients in this state. They may think that merely continuing with five-times-a-week analysis will be enough, but over the years I have become convinced that this is just not true, and many of these patients are hospitalized. So, I am simply suggesting that when any clinician sees this happening they should consider an intensified psychoanalytic approach rather than other interventions, such as medication or hospitalization, which would disrupt the analytic process and not provide them with what they need.

SB: Are you maintaining that a newly qualified clinician could do this? Don't you think that this kind of radical change in technique requires many years of experience?

CB: That depends entirely on the individual analyst. If anything, experience can lead to mental ossification and I am not sure that works in favour of helping these people. Although in a previous chapter, I indicated that, in principle, one need not be a highly experienced clinician to work like this, clearly a beginner might benefit from supervision, and certainly from collaboration. All recently qualified clinicians should, ordinarily, have supervision in such situations, unless they feel it would interfere with the unconscious communications of the patient with themselves. But all clinicians need a team of people or a highly competent psychiatrist to provide back-up for work of this kind. I was only about thirty-three when I worked with Emily, but I had already prepared for this eventuality by setting up a team. I therefore felt contained and somewhat assured that at least I knew what to do if extended analysis did not work. This did not make me confident, but it did allay those sorts of anxiety in the analyst that can interfere in work with people in breakdown. So, if a younger analyst has a patient who is fragile and likely to fall to pieces, then it seems wise to me that they should set up a back-up team, think through what extension of time would be likely to meet the patient's needs, and be sure to be there before the patient cracks up.

SB: So you do not think experience is a crucial factor?

CB: I think experience is important, but I object to the notion that analysts and therapists in their thirties are inexperienced or undeveloped. They will be adults, highly educated, and with life experience.

SB: You say that, although your all-day sessions have only ever lasted for three days, *in your mind* you are prepared to carry on working in this way for as long as it takes. Can you say more about this?

CB: In my own mind I need to be free of any pressure to 'get the job done' in a certain time. I could not function in the way I did otherwise. So I tell myself, and my patient, that we will work until we have seen them through their predicament. I convey to them that I am not going to give up unless their breakdown exceeds my capacity and that of those with whom I work, to help them through the ordeal. In the early days I did not know how long it would need to continue, but I found, to my great surprise and relief, that it did not take so long. I think this is because the patient's need functions as much on the symbolic level as the real. What they need is the symbolic commitment to a *potentially* indefinite period of work.

SB: You refer to your work as psychoanalysis but some of these patients have clearly been in once- or twice-weekly psychotherapy. Does this affect your approach when they are breaking down?
CB: No. A breakdown has its own logic and in my view its own special clinical demands. As long as one is prepared to provide sufficient analysis then my experience is that this will prove effective, whether the patient has previously been in analysis or in non-intensive therapy.

SB: There seems to be an irony here: that in these days of quick fixes promised by CBT, DBT and so on, you might be seen as doing the same thing.
CB: Well, that would be ironic indeed, but there are fundamental differences in perspective. Broadly speaking, the Freudian view is that a symptom or character disorder is *meaningful*. Painful though it is, the unconscious meaning resident in the symptom or the disturbed character trait, or in affective disturbances such as depression, must be given time to be understood. CBT and other forms of brief treatment are, in effect, cognitive analogues to medication. They aim to rid the self of the effects of the human dimension upon the self's consciousness. The psychoanalytical approach

certainly does, ultimately, aim to alleviate psychic pain, but not at the expense of meaning. At the time of the breakdown there is an almost overwhelming breakthrough of highly significant feelings, memories and thoughts. What I have found is that breakdown embodies its own logical process. If we go with this, the crisis passes and the patient emerges having changed. It is as if once the person feels safely held by the listening other they can release themselves to the total emotional experience, which they have been holding in abeyance. The truths that have been defended against are now free to saturate the person in highly overdetermined ways. The complexity of being human rushes in and overwhelms the previous defences; it is akin to a powerful natural event. Yet as soon as it is over this saturation with conscious meaning fades. People return to ordinary life and generally have few memories of the breakdown.

SB: You are very critical of CBT and DBT, implying that if they are employed with patients on the verge of breakdown that this will simply seal things over. Do you think of these increasingly popular forms of treatment as false cures?
CB: I am sure when used in certain circumstances they have a useful effect. If you take seminars or read manuals on the subject you will see that they are, in effect, common-sense self-help treatments. The course of therapy is begun by a clinician but the patient is given 'homework', so they resort to the teacher-pupil paradigm which I am sure does help some people. One of the reasons I think it is *so* popular is because it is the return of the uncanny; the sense that this *must* be right because there is a teacher and there is homework, so people can leave the adult world and return to school. Implicitly regressive approaches like this—that simplify the complexities of adult life—will always have an appeal. But short-term treatments of a person with a basic fault in their personality will not deal with the deeper issues, and I think today's enthusiasm for these treatments on cost-saving grounds can be dangerous.

SB: Yet it could be argued that you actually employ CBT-like techniques. For example, you give some patients a written description of their core dynamic. Does that not smack of a certain form of homework? Are you not utilizing the patient's cognitive abilities to focus on an educational document that is intended to effect change?

CB: In a certain sense I think CBT, DBT etc., have stepped into a vacuum left by psychoanalysis. I was trained in short-term or focal psychotherapy in Boston by Peter Sifneos, and in London by David Malan. I learned a great deal from them about how to focus on a core dynamic, why one should be lucid, and how and why one should stick to a dynamic explanation of what was taking place. My first psychoanalyst at Berkeley also worked in this way, perhaps unknowingly. He was very clear in what he said, and would repeat core interpretations that were memorable, and I found myself recalling them and using them during the course of the week. If this book, in part, restores to psychoanalysts the right to acts of lucidity, of focusing on core psycho-dynamics, then I see this as a good thing. And yes, there *is* something of the teacher-pupil paradigm in psychoanalysis, only here both are studying the analysand's unconscious productions and this is more of a partnership in facing the dynamic enigmatic.

SB: But you would not refer a patient in breakdown for CBT?
CB: No, absolutely not. That would be like telling a person with a major personality disorder that they will benefit from a course in common sense. It might be of some use, but it will not address the underlying situation, and their time will have been taken up in false hope. A similar thing happened during the golden days of EST, which drew hundreds of thousands of people to its praxis, ate up decades of people's lives, but did not transform their personalities. These techniques cannot, in my view, reach deeply into the heart of patients and help them with profound problems.

SB: This text is based on your personal experience with a small number of patients. In the age of evidence-based research what sort of proof can you provide for the efficacy of your approach?

CB: I am well aware of the marketing allure of the term 'evidence-based'; it's the traditional weapon of the social sciences against the humanities, but it irks social scientists that we can learn more about human beings from the individual example—from Shakespeare's *Hamlet*, let's say—than from the entire history of their carefully quantified contributions. Freud's method was humanistically based. He would study a single case—*Dora*, for example—and from the particular he would arrive at universal conclusions. His samples are hardly scientific, but therein lies their strength. The case of *Dora* is a single, shared object that anyone can read, critique and evaluate for themselves, from innumerable points of view. The social sciences take a different route: they accumulate data, test hypotheses, collate results and publish evidence. The trouble is that as this method severely restricts the range of possible variables it has to be extremely limited; it winds up examining and proving minute points that verge on the meaningless. This is categorically different from psychoanalysis. It would be like trying to compare two novels by counting up their respective numbers of commas, colons and question marks. That may perhaps be interesting to know, but does it address the essence of the novels? CBT has nothing to do with psychodynamics. It does not pretend to explore the mind. It simply offers short-term fixes for symptoms.

SB: Still, people reading your work are almost invited into a faith-based reading experience, are they not?

CB: I am not asking for belief from my readers. This book is the outcome of the lifetime experience of one psychoanalyst. It is presented in the hope that other people may want to explore for themselves the premise that psychoanalysis can enable a person to convert a breakdown into a breakthrough.

How such work is used and disseminated in the future will not be part of my experience. To have remained silent in the face of what I believe I have discovered might have been convenient—I hardly expect this text to serve me well with my colleagues—but I think I have no choice but to get it out there, and let others see what is to be made of it in time.

SB: You emphasize the care you put into setting up your team, the fact that it is accepted (if temporarily resisted) by the patient, but you rarely discuss the transferential aspects of the change of frame. I am not suggesting that you do not work with the transference (you clearly do), but your provision of what is in effect free treatment—extending the hours, sometimes even travelling to see the patient—these elements must surely have huge implications for the analysand's view of you.

CB: Not if the patient is in a breakdown. Let's imagine that you are swimming in the sea at leisure, a sailing boat passes by full of friendly people and they throw a ladder over the side and invite you to join them. That is, so to speak, an act of seduction and it will be clear to the person who accepts the gesture that they are taking part in a seductive moment. If, however, you are in the sea, drowning, and a lifeguard arrives and throws you a lifebelt, you will grab it as an instinctive act because it will save your life.

SB: But surely being saved brings an enormous transferential dimension? You are a saviour!

CB: No, I am a professional. A lifeguard may save a person's life but they have been trained to do it. It is their job. If they do what they are supposed to do then they will be effective. The drowning person may feel forever grateful to that lifeguard but it will not escape their mind that this is what lifeguards are meant to do.

SB: So you make a point of indicating clearly that this is a professional act and not an idiosyncratic feature of your emotional relation to the patient?

CB: Correct. I also regularly refer to myself in the third person—'your analyst thinks' or even 'your employee'—precisely in order to keep this knowledge alive. It is a professional relationship. I have been employed by this person to work with them, and my job is to analyse them. I will at times refer to myself as a third object from the beginning and throughout the analysis, whether I am dealing with a person in breakdown or not. Also, it helps to bear in mind that I am proposing myself as one figure within a group of people who will be helping the patient.

SB: Do you find that patients are surprised when you announce your new contract?
CB: No. I have not mentioned this and I should have, but when I propose the change of frame I always ask the person when they arrive to sit rather than lie down, if they are in analysis. If they are in psychotherapy I will begin by stating that I myself would like to start the session. So either way I provide them with signal anxiety, which means that I am now dealing with the higher level functions of their ego, because this is required by the task ahead. One is about to propose a change to the work, and I think the patient needs to resume the pre-analytic posture so that, symbolically, one can address their adult self.

SB: Isn't it shocking for them in a way?
CB: Only if you have misdiagnosed the situation. Remember, if the person is breaking down then the frame is already changing. You are trying at this point to provide a new frame; one that is more suitable to the degree of mental decompensation that presents itself to you.

SB: So the patient's breakdown is the definitive action that determines this?
CB: Yes, it is clear that there needs to be a different approach on the analyst's part. Many analysands actually think they are about to go to hospital, especially as often family or friends

are talking about this. The last thing they anticipate is that the analyst will suggest an intensification of the analysis.

SB: Is that explicit? Do you and the patient discuss hospital?
CB: No. Very rarely. I discuss the new guidelines and we focus on the new temporary frame.

SB: So it is conveyed that this is temporary?
CB: Absolutely. That is an important part of the temporality of boundary. By indicating that this is merely a temporary alteration of the analysis, until such time as the patient is through the breakdown and recovered, one helps the person to feel that ordinary life will return.

SB: You clearly feel that breakdown is a potentially transformative moment, be it negative or positive.
CB: Yes, very much so. It is actually a moment of great promise. A breakdown is the most powerful deferred action of a person's life. It brings with it a very intense combination of vulnerability, the desire for help and a willingness to cooperate in a new therapeutic alliance, together with a significant diminution of defences and resistances, a high degree of unconscious specificity in relation to the core problem and a new valuing of historicity. The self is flooded with sequelae of emotional experiences and you have an event with huge therapeutic potential.

SB: You distinguish between two separate origins of breakdown in the non-psychotic patient. Arguing from a classical Freudian perspective, you build a case for a form of mental fragility that derives from ego weakness, which is constituted out of the intrinsic challenges posed to all infants and small children, when the mind is insufficiently developed to deal with the force of the instincts and the difficulties of everyday life. The other situation is more in line with Ferenczi, Balint, Winnicott and others, for whom breakdown derives from failures in the self's early relationship to others.

What difference does the psychoanalyst see, if any, between these two very different paths to breakdown?

CB: The person who is suffering an *après-coup* that originates in parental or other early environmental failures will usually have organized into their historical narrative a sense of how they have been let down as children. They will demonstrate this in the transference, which will restage aspects of this early failure of the parental culture. So the analyst will have sufficient evidence from analysis of the transference, the countertransference and the free associations to allow them to locate the problem in the realm of the real; i.e. self to other. The other type of patient, one who is inherently fragile and self-limiting will not bring distinctive memories of the self's failure by parental others. Indeed, they may be very fond of their parents, who may continue to be of considerable help to them, and no such early trauma will be restaged in the transference. Instead, the analyst will find themself witness to a predominantly internal war going on between the drives and the self's mind; i.e. self to self. These patients will reveal mental structures predicated on particular psychodynamic axioms that have led to self-diminishing defences. In this case the *après-coup* is the trauma of the arrival of mental pain owing to long-standing structural issues.

SB: Do these two types of person present differently in other ways?

CB: People who are psychoneurotic (suffering from fundamentally internal wars) generally have a sense that there is something wrong with them, that they are the cause of their own difficulties; it is not something passed onto or into them from the other. These people are usually very clear that they cannot accept the generosity, love or interest of the other, because they would feel too internally disrupted. So they must refuse the other even as they are aware that acceptance of such invitations would be generative. They show the analyst that the battle is internal: for example, between sexual and aggressive drives, or between the threat of castration and the ambitions of desire. Or it may be between the superego, which they have invested with great power, and the self, which they see as a meagre mortal incarnation of imperfection. People engaged in such intense psychoneurotic conflicts have little time for others, and as children they may have caused much distress to loving parents, who simply could not reach them, much less help them to resolve their problems.

SB: In both situations, however, a breakdown is a deferred action?
CB: The psychoneurotic *après-coup* arrives in the analysis as the self rediscovers the mind's inability to deal with mental forces. The power of the drives is now met by the power of the superego, producing toxic forms of guilt, anxiety and depression that can be overwhelming. The analyst may have to function for some time as an auxiliary ego, enabling this person to deal with the trauma of having a mind in the first place. With the character-disordered self, on the other hand, the *après-coup* is the arrival of mental pain derived from the self's shocks in the real, but that does not mean necessarily with the parents. As discussed, a single small event in the real can have a profoundly distorting effect upon a person's self, and bias their character in a certain direction.

SB: Would you say, then, that with both types of personality in breakdown that you are, by extending the sessions, being an auxiliary ego?
CB: Yes, I think so. Paula Heimann, my first supervisor, used to make this point frequently. When I asked her why she was so interpretive, she maintained that by making an interpretation one was performing an auxiliary ego function. One had to recognize that people in analysis did break down because that was part of the effect of analysis; it is designed to intensify the conflicts in the self so that by illumination they could then be subjected to therapeutic transformation. So the

analyst had an ethical responsibility to step in and assist the patient by talking them through the situation they were in.

SB: That seems almost as if the talking cure is performed by the analyst!

CB: Yes, and in some respects, at certain times, that is absolutely true. During some breakdowns the analyst may, on balance, do more of the talking than the patient, especially when they are translating feeling states into words. (These can be feeling states in the patient, between patient and analyst, or in the analyst). On the other hand, one patient referring to our work said he thought psychoanalysis should not be termed the talking cure but 'the listening cure', which I think is most interesting and rather accurate.

SB: I suppose some of these patients would previously have been in child psychotherapy. Have you worked with people in breakdown who have had therapy as children and, if so, how does this bear on the outcome?

CB: I have worked with people who have been in child therapy and then proceeded in later life to have a breakdown. I find generally that if they were seen by a psychoanalyst in adolescence this can make an important difference to the working alliance in adult analysis. As adolescence is a representation of Oedipal and pre-Oedipal issues, if the patient remembers feeling helped by the previous analyst this will benefit them as they enter breakdown as adults. And as adolescence is its own form of breakdown they have had a type of rehearsal for the real deal; for breakdown later in life.

SB: In a previous work you wrote that when you interpret some patients do not appear to hear you at a conscious level, but that the interpretation still seems to serve as a catalyst for intense, creative thinking on their part. Is this a feature in working with people who are in breakdown?

CB: Yes. Lucid explanations, however brief, are rather like spoken reveries for the patient. They may not attend

particularly to the content—indeed, it may be entirely
forgotten—but the comments often seem to inspire their
thoughts to go in a new direction.

SB: How do you understand this?
CB: I think it is one form of unconscious communication
between the analysand and the analyst, as if the analyst's
commentary is a verbal matrix within which the patient can
imagine something completely different. It is, in Winnicott's
strict sense, a form of playing between the two. By 'playing'
in analysis, Winnicott did not mean that the two literally
played together but that the analyst's interpretations and the
patient's responses were, in themselves, a form of play. Lucid
interpretation, followed then by intermental activity, elicits
the *nature* of the patient's mental experience, and this is vital
to an understanding of their mind. As the reader will have
seen, at those points I tend to challenge the analysand's
mental axioms, and the analysand benefits from these
mentally engaging encounters with the analyst. The intention
is to introduce another perspective that loosens up the
patient's ability to engage in generative self-reflexivity. This
will be a temporary period in the work—sometimes just one
or two days—before such intense conscious activity subsides
and is forgotten, giving way to new unconscious axioms that
reflect the work that has been done.

SB: What do you think is the most mutative aspect of the
extended sessions?
CB: It is psychoanalytical time. The usual time frame set for
the psychoanalytic session is suited to social reality—it can
be fitted easily into the working day—but it is not determined
by the rhythm of the psychoanalytic process and it is not, in
my view, very well suited to the nature of unconscious life.
By extending a session to ninety minutes I think the analyst
adapts the frame to the possibilities of the unconscious. And
if one takes an entire day then the social realities of the two
participants have really been set aside in the interests of

psychoanalytical time. What has been surprising to me and to my patients is how natural this adaptation seems to feel. It is as if one were simply giving to the unconscious what it needs to do its work within the psychoanalytical experience.

SB: So you are saying that the conventional psychoanalytical frame is not suited to the full possibility of the psychoanalytical experience?
CB: Probably, yes. But we have to live with this limitation. I have felt thousands of times over my career that a session had ended too soon and that the analysand needed more time to gain deeper access to their unconscious. It is simply impractical to have such extended sessions on a regular basis, but in this sense perhaps we do fail to realize the real potential of psychoanalysis.

SB: Have you ever given extended sessions to a patient who was not having a breakdown?
CB: I think quite a few analysts will provide ninety-minute (or double) sessions under certain circumstances. For example, if a patient is travelling from abroad and can only have a brief period of analysis, or sometimes when working with a person who is very disturbed right from the beginning I might see them for ninety minutes. And for initial consultations I always offer a ninety-minute session, or even several sessions, before making a recommendation.

SB: Have you ever worked with anyone for an entire day that wasn't having a breakdown, simply to see if you could gain increased access to their unconscious life?
CB: No. I am intrinsically careful and I would not want to establish that as a precedent. Obviously one could not sustain this kind of work, and if it was offered at the start then it would then be experienced as the frame, the axiom of the analysis. I do not see how you could go from there to ordinary sessions afterwards. Also, it is important to emphasize that the all-day sessions only worked in the way they did because

of the previous period of analysis, and the fact that the patient was in breakdown and, therefore, in a deeply communicative state of mind.

SB: Returning to psychoanalytical time, is that the only mutative dimension to the transformations that are taking place in these analyses? You have discussed the role of consciousness and intermental work. What else would you add?

CB: There are many other aspects, of course. In breakdown the unconscious is more open, more specific, and there is also an urgent desire to return the self to a state free from mental pain. Two pasts become integrated—the immediate precipitating event and the density of the self's past—and this illuminates the structure of the self's breakdown. The logic of breakdown is revealed and can be explained. A *history* is created that links the two pasts. The process of putting these pieces of the puzzle together creates a new scaffold for the arrival of withheld affects, which now emerge as a full and powerful emotional experience. So, one has a more deeply contributing unconscious; histories that reveal the logic of breakdown and constitute a new gestalt. The self transforms from its previous pattern in being and relating to a new pattern. The old pattern had never been understood; it was ego-dystonic, the cause of great mental pain, even though it may have provided secondary gains such as masochistic pleasures. Now the self has an intense need for change, and this unconscious motivational shift overrides resistances and certain defences. As the new structure is developed through the analytic work it functions initially as a transitional psychic structure that is psycho-logical; it makes sense to the person. Such new-found sense is liberating, it is a relief, and gradually it becomes part of the individual's personality.

SB: How much change are we talking about? Surely you do not think the entire personality is affected?

CB: Of course not. Only the factors that contributed to ego weakness or mental fragility; the causes of the breakdown.

Afterwards when the person returns to ordinary analysis they will be able to work on other issues. If they are psychoneurotic then the breakdown and transformation will have been very significant as a measure of psychic change. If they are more disturbed, with a serious character disorder, then this will only be partly the case and much more work will be needed.

SB: If we imagine for a moment that your approach were to become standard practice, how could this be introduced to analysands and to the public?
CB: You appreciate that I think that is a stretch of the imagination. I do not anticipate that my colleagues will agree, for the most part, with what I have proposed. I would not recommend that analysts discuss this idea at the beginning of an analysis, although I suppose that if the patient had already heard about it then it could be confirmed as a measure to be used under special circumstances. This would no doubt have a certain meaning for the patient, and that would need to be analysed.

SB: You and David Sundelson have written a book on confidentiality, *The New Informants*, in which you advocate a policy of non-compliance with anyone seeking information on your patients. How do you reconcile these views with your use of a team?
CB: In *The New Informants* we argued that confidentiality was held not only by the psychoanalyst but by the profession. This enables an analyst to confer with other analysts about the patient. With people in breakdown I speak about the patient with the other professionals involved, but only in order to ask for their help. I do not discuss the patient or what is taking place in the analysis in any detail, and I provide their names only after receiving their permission to do so.

SB: But surely there must be pressure from your colleagues to tell them about what is going on that warrants such interventions?

CB: Yes that is true. I may state something objective, that the patient is in an 'agitated depression', for example, because I would want the psychiatrist to know the situation. The only real difficulty I have had with this has been in America when a patient is in marital therapy. In the United States, marital therapists regard it as normal practice to confer with psychoanalytic colleagues who are working with one or other partner in the relationship. Although they will have 'informed consent' to do so, and even though they will protect confidentiality in other respects, I am not comfortable with this way of practising. I think that, as far as possible, whatever one learns about one's patient should come from the patient and not from any other source.

SB: You seem fairly certain that your analytical colleagues will not approve of this book, but isn't it quite possible that more people practise along these lines than you know?
CB: I know that analysts do sometimes provide longer sessions and additional sessions. I have written this book in order to report on my own particular experience in this area, specifically that extended psychoanalysis be considered as an alternative form of treatment for people who are breaking down.

SB: Do you know of anyone else who has worked with a patient all day for several days in a row?
CB: No, I don't. But analysts may not be confident in reporting their work because of the ruling orthodoxies. It may well be that this has gone on and that people have had clinical success but have just not reported it.

SB: You wrote that you do not agree with aspects of Winnicott's technique, that he encouraged too much dependence on himself in the transference, and you emphasize the need to support the patient's ego health and to try and keep the patient functioning in reality. Could you say more about this?

CB: I think Winnicott went too far. Although I know from many people that he helped them very much, they were well put together people to begin with, so they could go through a Winnicottian experience and come out the better for it. But he did encourage patients to break down for the sake of it, and in some cases I think he was prepared to see it as ennobling that a person had found their own sense of inner personal reality, even if it meant they had virtually ruined their lives. It is as if he saw the breakdown as a sort of romantic idyll; two Neoplatonic beings inhabiting a rarefied place, with the urban world and external reality a long way away. I think breakdown is a tragedy, but when it comes— and it must come to you, you cannot force it as Winnicott did—it can be transformative. The analyst must know both how to be silent and receive the unconscious communications, and how to enter the patient's language and history with lucid comments that analyse the meaning of the breakdown. In other words, they must be able to operate within both the maternal and paternal orders.

SB: You set great store by the analysand's unconscious knowledge.
CB: The self hears from its unconscious. Like reading a book or being read to, it is deeply informative. Of course the analyst too needs to hear from the analysand; they then benefit from the accumulation of knowledge in the 'storehouse of ideas' to which Freud refers.

SB: So understanding the contents of the mind is important to work in this area?
CB: It is crucial, as these contents are the crystallized story of the self's ailment: the history of the mental issues and conflicts that brought the person to the point of breakdown. I want them to hear from them first, before they hear from me. I want them to learn from their own unconscious selves what they know. If one can help them get to that knowledge then the truth will set them free.

SB: How does this emphasis on free association come into play, practically speaking, when a person is in breakdown?

CB: By that time, hopefully, the analysand will have developed sufficient regard for their sequences of thought so that, even amidst great anguish and distress, when a pattern emerges the chain of ideas will function almost as a revelation.

SB: In *The Infinite Question* you discussed the interrogative drive. You suggested that both in dreams and in the narrative of a session, the person poses questions and then, often unconsciously, provides answers that are deeply relevant to the self, and that then lead on to further questions. When someone is in breakdown does the analyst represent some special unconscious function in that moment?

CB: For the French, the unconscious takes the function of the mother. It is a form of intrasubjective object relation. I believe that the self turns to the mother-unconscious in breakdown, and the thoughts that emerge are deeply prescient and valuable. In some respects, I think that at this time the analyst, in the transference, is both the arrival of the mother-as-container and the mind. It is as if the self returns to the being from whom the mind originated.

SB: You have written about 'broken selves', people whose previous breakdowns were not adequately met by a therapeutic other. This is not a common term and I wonder if you could say some more about it.

CB: I think there are many people who have had a breakdown at some point. No one was there to receive it, they recovered from the event, but it was lost on them and there was no breakthrough. Furthermore, the damage to a person of such a failure is inscribed in their being for the rest of their life. Even if they have averted a psychotic breakdown, they cannot conceal a feeling of having been deeply let down in their moment of crisis. It is probably most common when a person is rejected in a love relation. Rejection by a love object is horrifying. And often the self is bewildered, reluctant to take up further pursuits in this respect, and may live in what John Steiner terms a 'psychic retreat' for the remainder of their lives. This might look like chronic depression or a kind of low-level but persistent bitterness.

SB: You are not, then, putting a diagnostic tag on this? You seem to be implying that, whatever the person's diagnosis, if they have not had a previous breakdown they are better off than someone else with a similar diagnosis who has. This is because the first breakdown is likely to have caused a sealing over of the self, leading to a new kind of isolation.

CB: Yes, that is well put. There is a new layer of defensiveness, one predicated on the assumption of being failed by the other, and if this has been a significant part of their early history it will only add to that conviction.

SB: But presumably they can still be reached in analysis or therapy?

CB: That depends on the patient. Some are so defeated that they enter a stalemate with the analyst. All they can do is project their sense of despair into the analysis, forcing the analyst to repeat their fate. Other patients can be coaxed out of their psychic retreat back into some cathexis of the object world. Here, that distinction between the life and death instincts is so important. Those who are predominately under the sway of the death drive are unlikely to be reached. Those who still have life coursing through their veins can make progress.

SB: You mentioned that there were patients that you failed early on in your career, by not acting sooner to help them as they were breaking down. This might give the impression that, at some later point, you perfected your technique and had no further difficulties. For example, you say that no patient has needed hospitalization. Are you claiming that you have made no errors?

CB: No, of course not. I don't always get it right. For example, there were several occasions when I offered extended sessions to people who probably could have managed to work through the crisis with standard analysis. I also once offered all-day sessions to a patient for whom, in retrospect, extended sessions would probably have worked rather better. He was not distressed by the attempt, but after one day I told him that I thought we should return to a less intensive frame. It was important that we were able to analyse why I had thought he needed more intensive work.

SB: So, you subjected your recommendation to analysis?
CB: Yes, of course. But I would hope that all clinicians will at times analyse the analysis. We make a lot of mistakes, and these must be analysed in order for the process to work.

SB: Are there any other common problems?
CB: One difficult issue is the patient who is in a failing or malignant marriage, and whose partner is playing a central role in the collapse of the patient. If they are still living with the partner then I think three all-day sessions will not work. At most one should see the patient five times a week, with increased psychiatric intervention if necessary.

SB: The reader may wonder why you waited some thirty years before lecturing on this way of working. During this time, did many of your colleagues in London know that you took people into all-day sessions?
CB: None of my colleagues knew. For the first twenty years I simply made these adjustments when they seemed necessary, for the reasons explained in the text, but it was such a small part of my practice that I did not give it a lot of thought. But I was also aware, of course, that it would, or could be controversial and I wanted to gain more experience with it before sharing it with others.

SB: It would be interesting to know more about the effects this way of working has on you, as the analyst. Let's talk about concentration. How do you prepare yourself for an all-day session?

CB: In the morning I take plenty of time—an hour or so—before the patient arrives to prepare the room. I find this strangely comforting. If I am in a hotel suite in a foreign city then I will set up the couch with my chair behind it out of sight, so this involves moving furniture. I also set out the bottles of water on a side table within view of the patient. And then, for about half an hour before the session, I just sit in my chair and relax before going to the waiting area to greet the patient. I think what I do must be a form of meditation, or calming of the self.

SB: Do you not find the prospect rather daunting?

CB: No, not any longer. There is no need to feel anxious because I trust the process and the group of people with whom I am working with the patient.

SB: But *all day*? What is it like to sit in a room with a patient from nine to six?

CB. It is curiously very satisfying. This may sound strange, but there is something about the time of day—literally—that is part of the structure of this process. One begins with morning light and the sounds of the morning. There is something very optimistic about the morning; even the person in breakdown usually feels this. Then the sun begins to break down the morning and by midday there is an intermediate period of some hours that is looser, and this filters into the session. Then by three or four in the afternoon there is a feeling that one is winding down. The dusk carries us into a different mood.

SB: How many breaks do you take?

CB: I only take the lunch break. Otherwise I sit in the chair the entire time. Although the patient will take breaks I never have. I don't know why, other than that the entire experience, from beginning to end, is deeply meditative, and I do not feel like moving about.

SB: So, the final question. If you had to put this book in a nutshell, to sum it up for a newly qualified clinician maybe, what would you say?

CB: Trust in the method of psychoanalysis. Assemble your own team of fellow practitioners to help you, and be sure to catch the patient before they fall into decompensation. Simply extend the amount of the analysis and make certain you are clear about the agreement and the details of the extension. If it does not work, then the psychiatrist will assume clinical responsibility, and you will know you have done the best you could to meet your patient's needs.

Notes

Introduction

1 'Dr Branch' is a pseudonym, as he was so instrumental in our work together that the revelation of his name would jeopardize many patients' right to confidentiality.

1 Broken selves

1 See Rosenfeld, Herbert, 1987. *Impasse and Interpretation*. London: Routledge.

2 Signs of breakdown

1 See Bollas, Christopher, 2011, Character and interformality. In: Bollas, Christopher, *The Christopher Bollas Reader*. London: Routledge, pp. 238–248.

3 The guidelines

1 See Bollas, Christopher, 1992. Psychic genera. In: Bollas, Christopher, *Being a Character*. London: Routledge, pp. 103–145.

5 Anna

1 For those interested in reading about the history of this most remarkable psychoanalytic hospital in the United States, see Kubie, Lawrence S., 1960. *The Riggs Story*. New York: Harper & Brothers.

2 I always provide ample water. In great distress people are easily dehydrated so it is of benefit in that respect, but is also an important symbolic provision during this period of analysis.
3 Winnicott viewed aggression as akin to mobility. It was an indication of the self's ability to utilize the object in an essential and necessarily ruthless way; a means for the true self to be itself in the midst of relational niceties.

7 Histories and the *après-coup*

1 See Bollas, Christopher, 1995. The functions of history. In: Bollas, Christopher, *Cracking Up.* New York: Hill & Wang, pp.66–100.
2 See Bollas, Christopher, 1989. Historical sets and the conservative process. In: Bollas, Christopher, *Forces of Destiny.* London: Free Associations Books, pp. 193–210.
3 The term 'free listening' was coined by Adam Phillips and I have adopted it. See Phillips, Adam, 2002. *Equals.* London: Faber & Faber, p.31.
4 The concepts of preconception, realization, and conceptualization were formulated by Bion, and I use them here for my own purposes.

8 Time

1 Freud, Sigmund, 1923. Two encyclopaedia articles. In: Freud, Sigmund, *Standard Edition of the Complete Psychological Works of Sigmund Freud,* XVIII. London: Hogarth Press, pp. 233–259.

10 Reflection, explanation and working through

1 See Bogdan, Radu J., 2000. *Minding Minds.* Cambridge, MA, London: MIT, p.3.
2 See Hirsh, James, 2003. *Shakespeare and the History of Soliloquies.* Madison and Teaneck, NJ: Fairleigh Dickinson University Press.

Bibliography

Balint, Michael, 1968. *The Basic Fault*. London: Tavistock.

Bollas, Christopher, 1989. *Forces of Destiny*. London: Free Association Books.

———,1992. *Being a Character*. New York: Hill & Wang.

———,1995. *Cracking Up*. New York: Hill & Wang.

———, 2007. *The Freudian Moment*. London: Karnac.

———, 2011. *The Christopher Bollas Reader*. London: Routledge.

Bollas, Christopher, and Sundelson, David, 1995. *The New Informants*. New York: Aronson.

Freud, Sigmund, 1923. Two encyclopaedia articles. In: Freud, Sigmund, *Standard Edition of the Complete Psychological Works of Sigmund Freud*, XVlll. London: Hogarth Press, pp.233–259.

Kubie, Lawrence S., 1960. *The Riggs Story*. New York: Harper & Brothers.

Phillips, Adam, 2002. *Equals*. London: Faber & Faber.

Rosenfeld, Herbert, 1987. *Impasse and Interpretation*. London: Tavistock.

Steiner, John, 1993. *Psychic Retreats*. London: Routledge.

Index

breakdown 124; relationship with conscious self 88, 95, 96, 97; relationship with precipitating event 74; response to shock 70–1; role of act of interpretation 73–4; in role of mother 128; search for empathic other 71–2; as source of creativity 96

United Kingdom: 'evidence-based' mandates 9; fewer regulatory restrictions 9; flexible workplace idiom 34

United States of America: fear of litigation 34; marital therapy and confidentiality 126; regulatory restrictions 9

unreality, sense of 44

unthought known 65, 72–3, 80, 83

Ur dream 24, 95

visions 42–3, 77

water, provision of 47, 53, 62–3, 131, 134

'Wednesday analysands' 6

Will, Otto, Jr. 11–12

Winnicott, D. W. 6–7, 17, 105, 106, 110, 122, 126–7, 134

withdrawal: agitation as form of 30; full 29; partial 28

words: as triggers 72–3

work: absorption in 39, 42, 50–1, 92; effect of extended therapy on 34–5, 36; inability to focus on 27

working through process 92–7